INVEST IN LIVING

GW00319853

HOME VEGETABLE PRODUCTION

by

DAVID N. ANTILL

EP Publishing Limited
1976

The *Invest in Living* Series

About the Author

David Antill, NDH, has been involved with horticulture all his working life. He attended Pershore and Somerset Colleges of Horticulture and went on to work in marketing gardening in the Thames Valley and the Vale of Evesham. Since gaining his National Diploma he has worked at Askham Bryan College of Agriculture and Horticulture near York, first as a Lecturer and then, since 1969, as Senior Lecturer in Horticulture and Horticultural Manager. His interest in home production was aroused several years ago when he was asked to judge local allotments. Since then, he has tried out his ideas in his own thriving vegetable garden, which is proof that about 300 square metres of land is enough to provide vegetables for the average family of four all the year round.

Copyright © EP Publishing Ltd 1976, 1977

ISBN 0 7158 0455 3

Published 1976 by EP Publishing Ltd, East Ardsley, Wakefield, West Yorkshire WF3 2JN

Reprinted   1977

Printed and bound in Brighton England by G. Beard & Son Ltd

Contents

Introduction

This book on outdoor vegetables sets out to help the uninitiated, but it is also hoped that those with some experience will find useful hints.

You will not find here information already available from a host of other sources. It has not been considered necessary to list the tools you will need —the subject has been amply covered elsewhere. Similarly, there is no discussion of the different varieties of each vegetable (information readily available in seed catalogues), nor is there repetition of the cultural instructions given on every seed packet.

What you will find in this book is how to save housekeeping money and improve the quality of your meals by producing vegetables all the year round as simply as possible from whatever space you have available—however limited that may be—without any frills, tricks or difficult crops.

No protection of any kind is necessary apart from a small cold frame, which may only consist of a sheet of glass held up by a couple of bricks, and a windbreak, and even these are not essential — there need be no capital outlay to commence growing.

The book is centred around the average family of four living in the average geographical location with average climatic conditions; those with larger or smaller families and those who live in favoured or harsh climatic areas should be able to adjust accordingly.

A wide variety of vegetables may be grown in the open virtually anywhere in the British Isles, the main restricting factor being altitude, particularly in the north of the country. Because of our favourable climate a choice may be grown all the year round—how wide that choice is, and the length of the season, will depend on the geographical location.

The book only considers amateur situations; besides saving money, it is hoped that vegetable gardening will prove an interesting pursuit and give much pleasure to those who take it up. Because of inflation and fluctuations in supply and demand, prices have not been quoted, but if the appropriate amount of money is placed in a box each time vegetables are harvested— instead of being bought from the shops—quite a surprise may be in store at the end of the year.

Note: The following terms will be used in the book.

Base dressing is fertiliser applied before the crop is sown or planted. **B.O.M.** is bulky organic matter. **Compost** is rotted waste and vegetable matter. **F.Y.M.** is farmyard manure. **Humus** is decayed animal or vegetable matter. **K** = Potash. **N** = Nitrogen. **P** = Phosphate. **pH** refers to soil acidity. On a scale 0–14, below 7 is acid and above 7 is alkaline. **Top dressing** is fertiliser applied to the soil around the plants.

Geographical Location

In order to adjust the advice given for the average geographical location to fit your own particular situation, you must consider frost, rainfall, site aspect and wind. These are the major factors as far as the amateur is concerned, though the difference in sunshine hours between one place and another can be proved to be important commercially, as can other factors. Quite obviously those living in the south have advantages as far as temperature is concerned over those living in the north; rather than giving southerners a great deal more choice from the staple diet point of view, this tends to mean that two crops may be grown in a season on a given area rather than only one, and so less area may be required to grow the same amount of crops.

The amateur has to settle for the site he or she has got, but appreciating the four factors will help decide the sowing and expected harvest dates of crops. For example, if you know that your garden is situated in a 'frost pocket', runner beans or marrows should not be planted until June. It must be realised that sites can vary considerably in this kind of detail even though they are only a mile or so apart—the weather on one side of a hill may be quite different from that on the other.

Rainfall varies throughout the country. Generally, the hills in the west receive considerably more than the flatter land in the east, but as with frost, local rainfall may vary considerably. Quite a low range of hills may create a 'rain shadow', so that the area behind them away from the wind direction may be considerably drier than the hills themselves. Gardeners soon become aware of local rainfall and those in drier areas need to think much more about conserving water.

There is nothing you can do about the aspect of your site, but understanding its advantages or disadvantages can help you to plan what to grow and when to sow or plant. The most favoured sites are those facing south, particularly if they are on a slight slope. Crops grown on these sites will have an advantage over others, particularly those on north-facing sites, because the land warms up more quickly in the spring and can often be cultivated earlier in the year. Everybody must have noticed how snow always lies longest on the north side of a hedge or plough furrow. Making a realistic appraisal of your site and recognising its limitations can save you many disappointments. For example, a north-facing site simply might not be suitable for outdoor tomatoes or sweetcorn, and an east-facing site may prove too cold for overwintering peas or certain varieties of broccoli. In these circumstances you must adjust your crops accordingly.

Wind is the one factor the amateur can do something about. Research stations have proved that protection from wind is most beneficial, increasing yields considerably. What is required is not a solid barrier, which produces turbulence, but a filter through which the air can pass, as shown below. A hedge is the long-term answer but as a temporary measure a slatted wooden fence or loose-woven hessian type material held on stakes or poles will serve the purpose. The artificial filters should have a 50% cover, as shown.

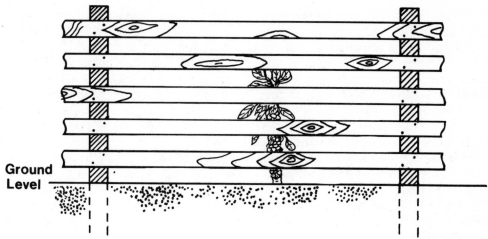

Front view of man-made windbreak (slatted wooden fence) showing 50% cover, 50% space

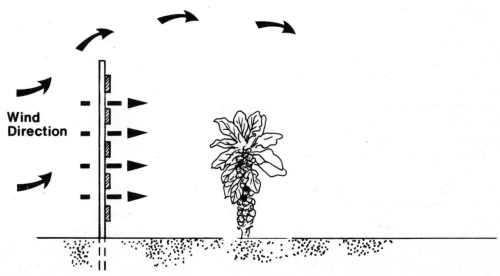

Section view. The hedge or man-made barrier must allow air to pass through it in order to avoid turbulence. The distance protected before the effect tails off is six times the height of the barrier

Site and Soil

Where site is concerned, amateurs usually have to accept the garden where they live, or an allotment close by, but where the vegetables are located in the garden can be important. Vegetables require full light—shade from trees or tall buildings reduces yields. This point cannot be emphasised enough. There are shrubs and flowers to be chosen that will flourish in shady places so keep the area in full light for the vegetables!

The soil that is on the site will fall broadly into one of the following categories: light sand, sandy loam, loam, medium loam, light clay, clay, silt and peats. Within these categories the soil will be of various mixtures, but all will grow perfectly satisfactory crops, provided they are treated in the correct manner. Sandy soils are generally referred to as light, loams as medium, and clays as heavy soils.

Because man has used them for a long time most old garden soils can be easily cultivated. Clay soils present the most problems as far as cultivation is concerned because of their 'sticky' nature—they can only be worked when containing just the correct amount of moisture. If worked when too wet they become a sticky mess; if allowed to dry out after rough digging and there is no frost, big hard lumps form. Knowing when to work the soil in the garden is dealt with on p. 27.

The texture of the soil depends on the size of the individual particles. Sandy soils have large particles, clay soils have very fine particles. The structure of the soil depends on how the individual particles bind together. It is therefore quite possible to have a sandy soil which binds together into rock-hard lumps to give a poor structure; this type of situation can be as bad as a sticky clay soil. Appreciating these points will help in deciding when cultivation can take place.

The addition to the soil of humus (decayed animal or vegetable matter) in all its various forms, including roots and tops of cleared crops, will improve soil structure. Soils with a poor structure (as those mentioned above) can also be improved if you go onto them only when the amount of moisture present is at its optimum and allow them to 'weather' after digging. The action of frost in particular, but also rain, wind and sun, will leave the soil structure in a good condition. That is why it is important that these more difficult soils should be dug in autumn roughly, left until spring and then cultivated when soil moisture is at its optimum.

The top-soil and the sub-soil should not be unduly mixed. The depth of top-soil is usually about 300 mm, but if the top-soil is insufficient in depth humus can be added to the sub-soil—over a period of time the depth of top-soil will be improved, as will the condition of the sub-soil.

New gardens that have been compacted by builders, and where soil levels have been altered, often present a real problem. The only way to start is to dig 300 mm deep, forking up the sub-soil, then leave the soil rough and allow it to weather over winter.

Drainage

However good the soil is it is useless for vegetables if the drainage is poor. There are several factors that can cause this problem. Simply a blocked drain is the first thing to look for, in which case the remedy is simple. Another possible cause is compaction, which can be solved by double digging. It may be a pan that has formed near the soil surface through chemical action—again double digging may solve it. These three factors can be solved on site, but the problem may be the result of ditches or drains outside the garden being blocked and this can only be solved by finding out whose responsibility they are. If you have the problem of poor drainage, do persevere until it is solved. Vegetables must have good drainage.

Rotation and Planning

These two topics are so closely related as far as the amateur is concerned that it is best to discuss them together.

The discipline needed to rotate crops successfully in a garden is difficult—and the smaller the garden the more difficult it becomes. Why is rotation necessary?

The main reason is that different groups of crops have different soil-borne pests and diseases. By not growing one of these groups on the same area for two years in succession, therefore, it is hoped that a build-up of these problems can be prevented. Rotation is more a means of prevention than a means of control—many of the soil problems, once established, can remain dormant in the soil for many years, and only 'spring to life' again when chemicals excreted from their host crop appear. As always, the problem is not a simple one because many of the soil-borne pests and diseases have weeds as alternative hosts.

It is much more necessary to rotate some groups of crops than others because some have few if any apparent soil problems; in some cases this may be due to the fact that they are only in the soil for a short time, not long enough for a particular pest or disease to build up. The crops that fit into this category can be planned to make sure that the others which do need the rotation are given it. This does not mean that it is wise to grow any crop year after year on the same area. All crops should be rotated if possible, and it would be wrong to think of vegetables in total isolation. When rotation and planning are considered other crops such as strawberries, bush fruit and flowers must be included. The most useful rotations include these crops as well.

The aim should be to give as long a rotation as possible. Most gardeners are able to manage a four-year (or four-group) rotation. It does not always mean every group gets a four-year rotation if there are four groups. One of these groups may be in the soil for two years or more. The temptation is always to grow too many brassicas or potatoes and these are the two main trouble groups as far as vegetables are concerned.

In order to draw up a rotational plan for vegetables you must first decide what you want to grow. This is largely a matter of personal choice, as tastes vary so much, but economic factors are bound to be taken into consideration. Remember, however, that the one crop you leave out because it was so cheap last year may well be among the most expensive next year. It is even more short-sighted to grow only the crops that are very expensive because of shortages one year—not only may those crops become the cheapest the next year, but if the area put down to one vegetable is larger than that group's fair share in the rotation there is a risk of building up a soil problem, so that the crop cannot be grown at all in the future.

But having said this, the smaller the area of land there is available for vegetables, the more valuable that land is—when this factor has to be considered it is right to think about growing crops which give the best value return. An example is that a head of lettuce and a head of cabbage will often cost about the same to buy. The difference is that a lettuce requires 650 sq cm to grow, but a cabbage requires 1,450 sq cm—over twice as much area—and so for the very small garden this could be a consideration. The geographical location may also influence the choice; for instance, it is not sensible to try outdoor tomatoes on a windy, exposed site.

With the above factors in mind a list should be drawn up. The chosen crops should then be put into their various groups:

brassica group—broccoli, Brussels sprouts, all cabbages, cauliflowers, radishes, turnips, or any member of this family

legume group—broad beans, French beans, peas, runner beans

onion group—bulb onions, leeks, salad onions, shallots

'others' group—those crops which do not fit into any of the other groups, such as courgettes, herbs, marrows, sweetcorn, spinach

potato group—on its own

root group—beetroot, carrots, parsnips

salad group—cucumbers, lettuces, outdoor tomatoes.

Of these groups it is the brassica and potato that are the most important to rotate on as long a term as possible.

Roots and onions are often put together, as are salads and others—this will depend on individual taste, especially if your garden is not big enough to grow all the vegetables you would like. When the list and groups from the list have been drawn up, you may find that you have included too many vegetables from one group, so that the groups are unbalanced. Groups may be joined together if there are insufficient crops from each to make up a rotation area, provided the groupings are kept to for a period of years, but if one group is much too large it will have to be pruned.

To state the area an average family needs to produce all their own vegetables is difficult because every family eats varying amounts, but approximately 300 sq m should be enough if the land is free of perennial weed, pests and diseases. Those who are able to grow two crops a year from one area may require less. It is quite possible with the aid of storage to have available for the table home-grown cabbages (also without storage in most parts), carrots, bulb onions and potatoes all the year round. It is unlikely that anybody would actually want to grow only onions, carrots, potatoes and cabbages—but they could form a sound rotation.

There are a few varieties of crops which need not be thought of too strictly in their groups because they are grown at times of the year when the diseases or pests do not attack, the chief examples being early cauliflower raised in pots, radishes sown before the end of April, and transplanted spring cabbage.

Plans 1–8 are examples of programmes that could be followed with the crops described later. You will be able to adjust them to your own requirements by substituting crops of your own choice, but the examples should give some idea of the amount of produce that can be expected from an area. It is better to think of crops as covering areas than as growing in rows —they are only put in rows to give each plant an equal area and to make hoeing easy. Remember the examples are only diagrammatic; the important point is that each rotation section is of the same area.

As previously mentioned, vegetables from different 'groups' are sometimes joined together in one rotation area or section of the plot. For the sake of clarity, however, the heading given to each section names only the main group or groups to be grown in that area.

1   3 year rotation

Plot 3m × 3m, divided each year into 3 sections 3m × 1m

		Year 1 (shown)	Year 2	Year 3
Row 1	early lettuce followed by beetroot (2 sowings in March and April)			
Row 2	mid-summer lettuce (2 sowings in May and June)	**Salads**	**Roots and Legumes**	**Brassicas**
Row 3	spinach **Salads**			
Row 1	summer cabbage			
Row 2	Brussels sprouts **Brassicas**	**Brassicas**	**Salads**	**Roots and Legumes**
Row 1	early carrots followed by French beans			
Row 2	leeks	**Roots and Legumes**	**Brassicas**	**Salads**
Row 3	onions **Roots and Legumes**			

2   3 year rotation

Plot 3.5m × 4.5m, divided each year into 3 sections 3.5m × 1.5m

		Year 1 (shown)	Year 2	Year 3
Row 1–5	3 sowings of lettuce, early radish (Row 4)			
Row 6	block of sweetcorn	**Salads and others**	**Roots and Legumes**	**Brassicas**
Row 7–8	2 courgettes **Salads and Others**			
Row 1	½ row calabrese ½ row summer cabbage			
Row 2	1 row Brussels sprouts **Brassicas**	**Brassicas**	**Salads and others**	**Roots and Legumes**
Double Row	runner beans (or peas)			
Row 2	1 row carrots	**Roots and Legumes**	**Brassicas**	**Salads and others**
Row 3	1 row onions (or leeks) **Roots and Legumes**			

3   4 year rotation   Plot 6m × 6m, divided each year into 4 sections 3m × 3m

Brassicas and Early Lettuce	Early Potatoes and Legumes
Row 1 — 2 varieties of summer cabbage (to mature at different times) — radish sown between rows in April	maincrop peas sown in May — Row 5
Row 2 — ½ row summer cauliflower ½ row autumn cauliflower	second early peas sown in April — Row 4
Row 3 — lettuce – ½ row sown March, ½ April, winter cabbage planted end of June	early peas sown in March — Row 3
Row 4 — 1 row Brussels sprouts	2 rows early potatoes, the first row lifted to be followed by French beans — Row 2
Row 5 — ½ row purple sprouting ½ row broccoli	Row 1

Brassicas and Early Lettuce — **Roots**   **Early Potatoes and Legumes** — **Others**

Roots	Others
Row 1 — leeks	1 plant bush X X 2 plants bush marrow X
Row 2	courgette
Row 3 — bulb onions	X X X X 2 plants X
Row 4 — early carrots, followed by autumn lettuce	block of ridge cucumber
Row 5 — beetroot	X X X X X
	sweetcorn
Row 6 — bed of maincrop carrots	X X X X
	½ row lettuce sown early May
Row 7 — parsnips	½ row lettuce sown late May 1 row spinach (or more lettuce) —

Year 1 (shown)

Brassicas and Early Lettuce	Early Potatoes and Legumes
Roots	Others

Year 4

Roots	Brassicas and Early Lettuce
Others	Early Potatoes and Legumes

Year 2

Early Potatoes and Legumes	Others
Brassicas and Early Lettuce	Roots

Year 3

Others	Roots
Early Potatoes and Legumes	Brassicas and Early Lettuce

Notes: Brussels sprouts, broccoli and purple sprouting will not be cleared until March or even April, so the next crop in the rotation must be one that is not sown or planted until May or June, for example maincrop peas or runner beans. Leeks are sometimes not harvested until March and need to be followed in the next rotation by a crop sown or planted from April, for example broccoli. Spinach is only used as an annual crop in this rotation.

4

4 year rotation Plot 9m × 12m, divided each year into 4 sections 4.5 × 6m

Legumes	Brassicas
Row 1 — double row of runner beans	early summer cauliflower followed by lettuce — Row 1
Row 2 — early peas sown in March followed by lettuce	mid-summer cauliflower — Row 2
Row 3 — second early peas sown in April	calabrese — Row 3
Row 4	early summer cabbage — Row 4
Row 5 — 3 rows maincrop peas for fresh use and freezing	autumn cabbage — Row 5
	early planted lettuce followed by spring cabbage — Row 6
Row 6	Row 7
Row 7 — broad beans followed by overwintering salad onions	2 rows Brussels sprouts — Row 8
Row 8 — French beans	broccoli — Row 9
	winter cabbage — Row 10

Roots	Others and Potatoes
Row 1 / Row 2 / Row 3 / Row 4 — 4 rows bulb onions	outdoor tomatoes — Row 1
Row 5 / Row 6 — 2 rows leeks	bush marrows — Row 2
Row 7 / Row 8 — 2 rows parsnips	early potatoes — Row 3
	Row 4
	2 rows maincrop potatoes — Row 5
Row 9 / Row 10 — 2 beds (6 rows per bed) of maincrop carrots to lift for storage	salad onions ½ row sown April, ½ May; early sown lettuce followed by beetroot — Row 6 / Row 7
Row 11 — early carrots followed by over-wintering bulb onions	3 rows summer lettuce, ½ a row to mature at a time — Row 8 / Row 9 / Row 10
	autumn lettuce — Row 11

Year 1 (shown)

Legumes	Brassicas
Roots	Others and Potatoes

Year 4

Roots	Legumes
Others and Potatoes	Brassicas

Year 2

Brassicas	Others and Potatoes
Legumes	Roots

Year 3

Others and Potatoes	Roots
Brassicas	Legumes

Notes: Overwintering salad or bulb onions will not be cleared until April for the former and June/July for the latter. Examples of crops to follow are winter cabbage following salad onions and lettuce following overwintering bulb onions. Maincrop peas need not be sown until May, allowing overwintering brassicas to be cleared.

The diagrams on the preceding pages have shown ideas on how rotations can be integrated. There now follow ideas on basic rotations for larger plots, which offer more chance for integration. It is always advisable to use an exercise book and draw out the programme year by year, keeping a diary so that sowing and harvesting dates may be recorded. In this way adjustments can be made, to sowing dates in particular, to suit your own requirements. It will also help to keep the discipline required to stick to the rotations. For example, it may be that brassica and potato crops have been put in the same section for rotational purposes; on a four-section rotation it is then possible, if you keep proper records, to grow these crops on the same land only once in seven or eight years. This gives the soil an even better chance of staying free from the troublesome pests and diseases. An example of how to keep the land free of a particular crop for as long as possible is shown in Plan 6.

5 5 year rotation

Year 1	Year 2	Year 3	Year 4	Year 5
Potatoes	Others	Brassicas	Roots	Legumes
Legumes	Potatoes	Others	Brassicas	Roots
Roots	Legumes	Potatoes	Others	Brassicas
Brassicas	Roots	Legumes	Potatoes	Others
Others	Brassicas	Roots	Legumes	Potatoes

6

4 year rotation,
showing how to keep the land free of a particular crop for as long as possible

Year 1

Brassicas and Potatoes	Legumes
1 row Brussels sprouts 1 row cabbage/cauliflower 1 row broccoli 3 rows potatoes	double row runner beans 1 row broad beans 3 double rows peas
Roots	**Salads and Others**
4 rows carrots 2 rows parsnips 2 rows beetroot 4 rows onions 2 rows leeks	4 rows of lettuce to be sown in succession 1 row tomatoes block of sweetcorn block of marrow or courgettes

Year 2	Year 3	Year 4

Legumes	Salads and Others
Brassicas and Potatoes	Roots

Salads and Others	Roots
Legumes	Brassicas and Potatoes

Roots	Brassicas and Potatoes
Salads and Others	Legumes

The rotation is then repeated, but the crops within each section are switched, thus:

Year 5

Brassicas and Potatoes	Legumes
3 rows potatoes 1 row Brussels sprouts 1 row cabbage/cauliflower 1 row broccoli	3 double rows peas double row runner beans 1 row broad beans
Roots	**Salads and Others**
4 rows onions 2 rows leeks 4 rows carrots 2 rows parsnips 2 rows beetroot	block of sweetcorn block of marrows or courgettes 4 rows of lettuce to be sown in succession 1 row tomatoes

Years 6, 7 and 8 will then follow the same pattern as Years 2, 3 and 4, but with the crops within each section being arranged as shown for Year 5.

7

The following diagram shows how other crops may be used in a rotation

Year 1	Year 2	Year 3	Year 4
Rhubarb, Strawberries and Herbs	Rhubarb, Strawberries and Herbs	Salads and Potatoes	Roots
Brassicas	Legumes	Rhubarb, Strawberries and Herbs	Rhubarb, Strawberries and Herbs
Roots	Brassicas	Legumes	Salads and Potatoes
Salads and Potatoes	Roots	Brassicas	Legumes
Legumes	Salads and Potatoes	Roots	Brassicas

Year5	Year 6	Year 7	Year 8
Brassicas	Legumes	Salads and Potatoes	Roots
Roots	Brassicas	Legumes	Salads and Potatoes
Rhubarb, Strawberries and Herbs	Rhubarb, Strawberries and Herbs	Brassicas	Legumes
Salads and Potatoes	Roots	Rhubarb, Strawberries and Herbs	Rhubarb, Strawberries and Herbs
Legumes	Salads and Potatoes	Roots	Brassicas

Intercropping

Intercropping, if well done, may be of great value, particularly in the small garden, and will increase the potential output of a given area considerably. Timing is of the greatest importance for it to be successful. Before it can be practical a few points about the intercropping plan must be considered.

■ Does it interfere with rotation?

■ Is the manuring and fertiliser treatment suitable to both crops?

■ If spraying is contemplated against pests and diseases, will either crop suffer? An example of this problem: if one crop needs to be sprayed when the other is just ready for harvest, either the harvest or the spraying must wait.

■ Will one crop overshadow the other? This must be avoided. If one of the crops turns out a failure, the whole exercise has been a waste of time— it would have been better for two crops to have been grown consecutively.

Intercropping is normally most successful when long and short maturing crops are used or when one crop can be sown just before another crop is harvested. It is not possible to have two crops maturing at the same time and call it intercropping; the idea is to be able to take two properly full yielding crops in one season from an area of land that would normally only be able to produce one. Also, for the scheme to work properly, crops often need to be slightly farther apart than normal spacing would dictate. However, intercropping can enable many gardeners to produce three crops a year from a given area when only two would normally be possible.

Radishes are a good candidate for intercropping; they are normally eaten from April until July and it is usually possible to fit them in with other crops without having to give them an area of their own. The early sowings, which will not 'offend' the rotation problem, can be between rows of lettuce, onions or parsnips, the later sowings between rows of brassica plants on the brassica rotation.

Early lettuce, particularly the smaller varieties, may also be intercropped with long-growing crops such as parsnips and brassica plants. Runner and French beans may be sown amongst early lettuce and early cabbage just before these crops are harvested; in this way three weeks may be gained in the length of growing season for the beans.

The main disadvantages are:

(i) You must avoid damage to the remaining crop when harvesting the first;

(ii) There is an increase in hand weeding.

Note that in Plan 8 the distance between the end rows in adjacent sections will vary from year to year.

Basic 3 year rotation using intercropping

8 Plot 4·5m × 6m, divided each year into 3 sections 4·5m × 2m

Brassicas and Early Lettuce

- 150mm — 1 row Brussels sprouts planted early May
- 600mm — 1 row lettuce – may be 2 sowings but to mature by mid-June
  - ½ row cabbage planted mid-May; ½ row cauliflower planted mid-May
- 450mm — 1 row radish – may be 3 sowings, but to mature by end of May
  - ½ row cabbage planted mid-April; ½ row cauliflower planted mid-April
- 450mm — 1 row radish – may be 3 sowings but to mature by mid-July
  - early lettuce planted March followed by broccoli planted June
- 350mm

Roots and Legumes

- 100mm — 1 row salad onions sown in March
- 450mm — 1 row French beans sown in late May
  - 1 row early beetroot sown as early as possible
- 450mm — runner beans sown early June ⎯ ⎯ ⎯ ⎯
- 150mm — double row first early peas, to be harvested late June ⎯ ⎯ to form
- 600mm — runner beans sown early June ⎯ ⎯ ⎯ ⎯ double row
- 150mm — 2 rows early carrots followed by late peas
- 100mm

Sweetcorn, Potatoes, Marrows, Leeks and Late Lettuce

- 350mm
- 450mm — X X X X block of sweetcorn
  - 2 rows first early potatoes followed by leeks
- 450mm — X X X X underplanted by
- 450mm — X X X X trailing marrows
  - 2 rows second early potatoes followed by autumn lettuce
- 300mm — X X X X

Year 1 (shown)	Year 2	Year 3
Brassicas and Early Lettuce	Sweetcorn, Potatoes, Marrows, Leeks and Late Lettuce	Roots and Legumes
Roots and Legumes	Brassicas and Early Lettuce	Sweetcorn, Potatoes, Marrows, Leeks and Late Lettuce
Sweetcorn, Potatoes, Marrows, Leeks and Late Lettuce	Roots and Legumes	Brassicas and Early Lettuce

Basic Cultivation

Preparing for Digging

Basic soil cultivation is by far the most important aspect of growing vegetables. Many crop failures are due simply to inadequate or non-existent cultivation.

If you have a new or an old neglected garden, it is most important that any perennial weed that is present is eradicated. Weeds of this nature in growing crops will reduce yield because of competition for light, nutrients and water. It may be possible to clear the weed by hand if the problem is not too serious, though all the root must be removed or it will only grow again; if the infestation is light such weeds as dock, dandelion and couch grass can be dealt with in this way. Other weeds such as bindweed and creeping thistle are more of a problem and the use of chemicals may be necessary to obtain satisfactory control. Chemicals for this purpose are available to the amateur but the instructions must be followed precisely. The chemicals are normally applied in the spring or early summer while the weed is in maximum growth; the chemical is then translocated by the plant, which thus kills itself, though an interval of several weeks may elapse. See Weed Control, p. 39.

Turf must not be confused with perennial weed or couch grass. If dug in properly it is of great benefit to future crops.

pH or Soil Acidity

Before digging commences, the pH of the soil (it is always written with a small p and capital H) should be checked. The pH scale is from 0–14 and indicates the acidity or alkalinity of the soil; pH 7 is neutral, below 7 is acid, above 7 is alkaline. If a soil sample is taken, some chemists, for a small charge, will test it. A few horticultural firms supplying sundries also offer this service, and there are various kits on the market which enable soil testing to be done at home. These vary in accuracy, the more expensive kits normally giving a better result. It is possible to use litmus paper simply to test if the soil is acid or alkaline, but the results can be very inaccurate.

The pH for vegetables should be between 6.5 and 7.5. It is not likely to be above 8, but the addition of humus and use of sulphate of ammonia as a nitrogen fertiliser will help to bring the pH down if necessary. On the other hand it is quite possible that your pH reading could be low, so for every 0.5 that it is below 6.5 spread 0.25 kg per sq m of ground limestone (sometimes known as carbonate of lime) evenly over the soil at the same time as the base dressing is applied. This can then be worked into the soil. Before digging in the autumn after crop clearance, the dressing may be repeated if the required pH level is difficult to maintain.

Digging

Digging or rough forking may be carried out at any time of the year. Turning the soil is necessary for a variety of reasons: to add manure or bulky organic matter (hereafter referred to as B.O.M.) to the soil; to overcome compaction, so improving structure; or to allow weathering, so that a tilth can be more easily achieved ready for sowing or planting. Forking, provided it is done properly to a depth of 300 mm, is quite satisfactory when B.O.M. is not required. For crops which are sown or planted before the end of April, ideally it is best to dig the soil in the preceding November or December. This allows time for any B.O.M. that may have been added to rot down, and it is hoped that frosts in January and February will leave the top 150 mm of the soil in a fine condition for making a tilth. It is possible to dig some particularly easily-worked, well-structured sandy soils the day before sowing or planting in March or April,

but if B.O.M. is to be added the soil should be dug in November or December. B.O.M. that has not had a chance to rot down can for a time be toxic to plant roots. Digging in autumn can take place in fairly wet conditions without any harm being done. At this time digging in frost or a light covering of snow does not matter either, but frost should not be dug in during February, March or April—it may become sealed in and stay frozen for a considerably longer time below the surface than if left on it.

On soil where crops are not harvested until March, April or May, for example where broccoli and leeks have been grown, digging can take place as soon as they are cleared. If B.O.M. is thought to be required for the next crop, it should only be added if there is a time lapse of six or eight weeks before the next crop is to be sown, unless it is really well rotted. However, these over-

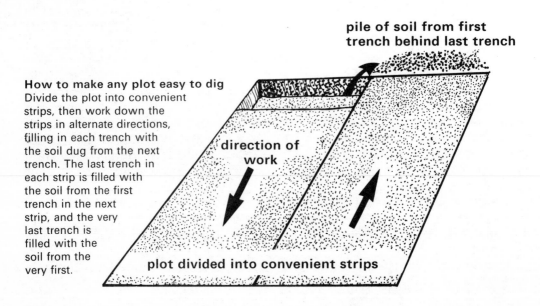

pile of soil from first trench behind last trench

How to make any plot easy to dig
Divide the plot into convenient strips, then work down the strips in alternate directions, filling in each trench with the soil dug from the next trench. The last trench in each strip is filled with the soil from the first trench in the next strip, and the very last trench is filled with the soil from the very first.

direction of work

plot divided into convenient strips

wintering crops can usually be followed by peas or maincrop carrots, for example, in which case no B.O.M. is required. A drawback to digging at this time of year is that the weather can be very dry. Digging exposes a large surface area to the air and the soil therefore dries out very quickly on top; with no frost it will often dry into hard unworkable lumps. When the addition of B.O.M. is not required forking is probably better than digging and if the weather is dry, treading the soil afterwards will form a cap over the soil surface that will conserve moisture in the soil. This is not to be confused

Single digging The trench is 300 mm wide and 225–300 mm deep. Annual weeds and B.O.M. are placed in the bottom of the trench as digging takes place

with 'capping' a seedbed, which must be avoided. It may sound contradictory to fork or dig to dispel compaction and then tread the soil down again, but the forking or digging is done to overcome compaction below the surface— most of the overwintering crops have been in position for a long time and the soil becomes consolidated. Any digging or forking carried out during the late spring and summer should not be left rough but chopped with the spade or fork as the work is done, as there will be

no frost to break the lumps of soil down.

Digging for crops to be planted in mid or late summer, for example spring cabbage or autumn lettuce, can include the addition of B.O.M., provided it has been stacked during the previous months so that it is very well rotted.

If you are unable to provide irrigation you should not be too ambitious in the amount of crops you attempt to grow from one piece of land in a year. It is possible, for example, to grow a crop of lettuce before planting broccoli in June, but if the weather is very dry at this time and the soil has been forked over after the lettuce crop—the crop of lettuce itself will have removed much of the soil moisture—establishment of the broccoli crop may be difficult. It is far better in these circumstances to prepare the tilth for the broccoli in April when soil conditions are just right, and to leave it uncropped until

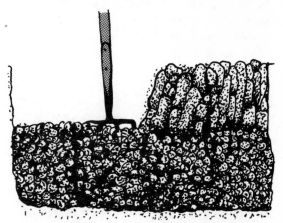

Double digging The trench is 600 mm wide, the extra width being necessary to allow free movement of the fork. The top 300 mm is turned as for single digging, but the bottom of the trench is dug with a fork to a further 300 mm before the next spit is turned. Annual weeds and B.O.M. are spread in the forked trench.

planting time in June. The tilth prepared in April will conserve the soil moisture (rather like moisture being conserved under a stone) and no matter how hot and dry the weather is at planting time the crop should establish and grow satisfactorily. This is known as a 'stale' seed or planting bed.

While digging, the soil should be kept level—hollows or bumps can lead to uneven drying-out of the surface. It may be necessary to dig or fork the sub-soil; most roots of vegetable crops will penetrate well into the sub-soil in search of moisture in particular, but this area must be free-draining and so 'sub-soiling' or double digging every few years is a sound policy, if it is possible.

It is not necessary to dig or fork the land after every crop in summer, though digging or forking should always take place after a long-term crop such as bulb onions, broccoli, or Brussels sprouts. In addition, the land has always been walked on considerably after these crops because of harvesting methods and so it will be compacted.

After a crop of early lettuce or early summer cauliflower, however, it may not be necessary, or indeed prudent, to dig or fork the land, particularly if the weather is hot and dry. Provided the soil has not been walked on too much, the second crop, such as beans or transplanted brassicas, can be sown or planted as soon as the first crop has been cleared; all that is required is a hoeing to uproot any weeds and a raking to remove the weeds and crop debris. If intercropping is being practised, then only hoeing can take place between the plants and the removal of debris must be done by hand.

Bulky Organic Matter (B.O.M.)

This refers to farmyard manure, shoddy, rotted straw, compost or any other organic waste material that will rot down. The material most commonly used by gardeners is farmyard manure (F.Y.M.). This is becoming increasingly difficult to obtain as newer farming techniques come into operation. Compost is probably the next most commonly used.

Making compost is not difficult and it can be a most useful way of getting rid of any organic material from the house or garden. Even brushwood that has been used to stake peas can be used, as well as such items as scraps of newspaper, grass mowings, and eggshells. One word of wording must be given at this point, however: any brassica stumps that have club root, potato haulm with eelworm, or grass mowings after a lawn has been treated with a selective herbicide should not be included, but burnt on a bonfire as an insurance against any carry-over of pest, disease or residual herbicide when the compost is used.

A compost heap should heat up considerably; though artificial help is not essential, the process may be aided and speeded up by sprinkling 125 g per sq m of straight nitrogen fertiliser onto the heap for approximately every 900 mm of unrotted waste until the heap is closed to mature. This heating process will kill many pests, diseases, weeds and weed seeds. When the heap is as high as can be conveniently managed—usually about 1.4 m—the top is sealed with 75 mm of soil; as the heap matures it will shrink considerably and approximately six months after sealing the compost can be used. Any unrotted

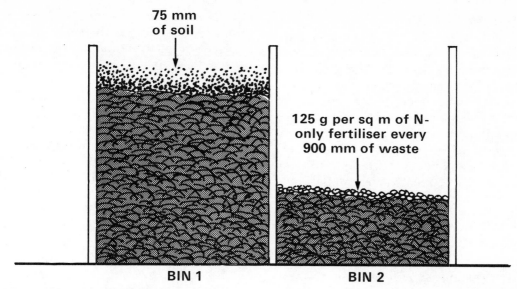

75 mm
of soil

125 g per sq m of N-
only fertiliser every
900 mm of waste

BIN 1   BIN 2

Compost bins   While bin 1 is maturing bin 2 is being filled. Bin 1 can be used about six months after the soil has been put over it.

material from the sides may be returned to the new heap. Some gardeners will have far more compost than others, and some heaps may take a whole year or more to reach the point of sealing, but this does not really matter. The area the compost heap takes up will also tend to be proportional to the size of the garden, but at least two compost heaps are necessary so that one can be filled while the other is maturing.

When there is to be a time lapse of six or eight weeks until the next crop in summer or an overwintering period, green material can be dug or forked into the soil where it will rot perfectly satisfactorily. The compost heap is simply a convenient way of reducing the bulk of green material and provides somewhere to put it when it is not convenient to dig it in. The above diagram shows the making of a compost heap.

No B.O.M. has a very high nutrient value and it cannot fully replace fertilisers. The different forms vary considerably in nutrient and humus value, but their chief purpose is to improve soil structure. An average application rate is approximately 10 kg per sq m, which has an effect for about two years. If you are confronted with a really sticky clay, the structure can be improved by the addition of coarse sand or even weathered ashes as well as B.O.M. Peat is a most useful agent in improving soil structure, and will also help to reduce pH if this is high. It has not been mentioned with other B.O.M. because it is usually comparatively expensive; anybody who has a source of supply is in a fortunate position. However, a dressing of peat becomes ineffective fairly quickly because the soil bacteria soon break it down.

Fertiliser

So far digging, B.O.M., pH and clearing perennial weed have been discussed. It can now be assumed that the soil is ready for breaking down to a tilth. Before this commences the amount of fertiliser required needs to be considered, and to do this a few important points must be made and understood. The importance of keeping nutrients up to the correct level cannot be stressed enough. The only satisfactory way of achieving this is by adding fertiliser to the soil; yields high enough to make worthwhile the effort and time spent on cultivation cannot be expected unless this level is maintained each year.

Many elements are required. Those used by plants in very small quantities are called 'trace elements', and soils are normally able to supply these on a permanent basis; only occasionally do they have to be added by man. It is the three major elements required as nutrients, i.e. nitrogen, phosphate and potash (known as N, P and K) which need to be applied each year, though some soils prone to acidity (low pH) also require calcium in the form of ground limestone, as already discussed. P is required by all crops in constant amounts. N and K are required by different crops in varying amounts, and have an influence on each other, so the amount of fertiliser applied must have the correct ratio of N to K for each crop or group of crops.

Generally speaking, leafy crops such as brassicas require more N than K, while root crops require more K than N. Beans and peas are able to 'store' N from the soil in small storage cells called nodules on their roots, so they do not require as much N as K. During their early growing season, onions and leeks require more N than K.

Over-riding the above considerations is the time of year. N produces lush soft growth, while K makes plants' growth tough and hard. It is therefore important not to give plants too much N immediately before winter because they will be unable to withstand the colder weather. Crops, rather like humans, require a properly balanced diet of nutrients in order that growth can be properly balanced.

To fulfil the needs of vegetables, two types of fertiliser are required. The first is a compound fertiliser containing N, P and K. They should be contained in the fertiliser in approximately the following ratio: 15%N : 10%P : 20%K (this will vary slightly according to the manufacturer). As a basic minimum each year, 85 g per sq m of this fertiliser will be required for *all* vegetable crops, applied before they are planted or sown.

The second fertiliser required contains N only; usually there is approximately 20%N in the fertiliser.

Amounts of fertiliser needed by each crop vary—some only require the minimum compound fertiliser, others require more, plus the N-only one as well. Amounts for each crop or group of crops are discussed for each crop separately in the list starting on p. 45.

The buying of fertiliser is often a problem. The compound described above is the ideal one to use but is not always available to the amateur. A straight N-only fertiliser is more easily acquired, usually in the form nitro chalk, but as referred to under pH may also be sulphate of ammonia. A widely used compound fertiliser is 'Growmore', which contains 7%N : 7%P : 7%K, but as the percentages show, two or three times the normal amount of fertiliser is required to give the correct amount of nutrients. Even then, because it is a 1N : 1P : 1K ratio it is not really satisfactory and can only be made so by the addition of N-only or K-only fertilisers.

It is possible to make up your compound fertiliser by using fertilisers that contain one nutrient only. The following are usually available: nitro chalk, containing approximately 25%N only; superphosphate, containing approximately 18%P only; sulphate of potash, containing approximately 48%K only. By using these, any type of compound fertiliser in any ratio of N, P and K may be made. For example, to make up a base dressing high in K for roots, i.e. 1N : 1P : 1½K, similar to the compound fertiliser recommended earlier, the following amounts per square metre are required: 50 g nitro chalk, 75 g superphosphate and 40 g sulphate of potash. If a base dressing high in N is required for brassicas, i.e. 1½N : 1P : 1K, the rates per square metre are 75 g nitro chalk, 75 g superphosphate and 25 g sulphate of potash. Nitro chalk can also be used as an N-only top dressing.

There are other fertilisers available such as dried blood (mainly N), hoof and horn (mainly N) and John Innes Base, which is a compound fertiliser— these are good but very expensive and so are usually restricted to glasshouse crops. It is most important to keep the unit cost as low as possible. Ground limestone, referred to under pH (or carbonate of lime), is also readily available.

It is always better to buy in bulk. If kept completely dry, fertiliser will store for several years. To buy in bulk it may be necessary for several people to club together or, better still, you could join a horticultural society or similar organisation. The subscription involved is negligible compared with the amount of money that can be saved, as all properly-run societies are able to buy in bulk and distribute to their members. This will also apply to other sundries, for example, peat, seeds, canes, etc.

Preparation of the Soil for Sowing or Planting

Once the amount of fertiliser required has been worked out, it should be spread evenly over the soil, which can then be broken down with a fork and finally with a rake to form a tilth. The act of breaking the soil down works the fertiliser into the soil to a depth of about 100 mm. Knowing when it is dry enough to walk on the soil to do this operation can only come with experience of each garden. A good guide is that if the soil sticks to the underside of your boots when you walk on it, it is too wet—patience, particularly in the early part of the year, can save a great deal of inconvenience later on. Walking on the soil when it is too wet will destroy all the weathering that has taken place and cause compaction; crops will suffer because their root systems will not be able to penetrate the compacted soil. Wait until conditions are just right.

There are a few crops which need to be planted early in order to gain maximum yield; for example, onions from sets, which should be planted in February. If the soil is still wet by the end of February, a large enough area for this crop can be broken down by working from planks of wood—the planks disperse your weight so that compaction is avoided or kept to a minimum.

The timing of cultivation is important. There are no short cuts. In the spring it is best to break down the overwintered digging as the opportunity presents itself, even if it is still several weeks away from sowing or planting time— the land will then be ready in time for the sowing or planting operation, which again can be done from planks if necessary. Sometimes your patience will be driven to breaking point, but it is always rewarded in the end. Nature has a remarkable way of righting itself if crops are not sown quite on time.

The difference between 'firming' the soil and 'compacting' it must be understood. Only very few crops require unfirmed soil; when the soil is at the correct moisture level (not so wet that you are having to work from planks) it should be firmed by treading. Knowing how much firming should be done can only come with experience. It is quite impossible to describe all the various combinations of soil moisture level, the type of soil and how many times it needs to be trodden to achieve the optimum result! There are one or two guide-lines to help, however.

After firming it should be possible to push the full depth of your forefinger into the soil without feeling any hard lumps or the hole collapsing when the finger is withdrawn. Alternatively, if a hole 100 mm deep is made with a trowel, the sides of the hole should not fall in when the trowel is withdrawn, but neither should they be smeared; if the hole collapses, the soil is not firm enough, and if the sides are smeared, the soil has either been worked when it was too wet, or firmed too hard.

It is very difficult to be able to arrive at ideal soil conditions every time, but if the ideal is aimed for although not always quite achieved, crops will grow satisfactorily.

A stale seed or planting bed (as described on p. 24) is always an advantage to the amateur. It will last for up to four months and can be sown or planted at any time during that period; it conserves moisture, and a shallow raking 50 mm deep immediately before sowing or planting will destroy germinating weed seeds, so allowing the crop to start without competition.

When the soil has been broken down, the top 100 mm should have no hard lumps which roots are unable to penetrate, but be of an even texture throughout.

Propagation

While bearing in mind that this book is concerned only with growing vegetables in the open, it is necessary to discuss the raising of plants in a simple cold frame, besides considering seed sown outside in drills. The construction of a cold frame is shown below.

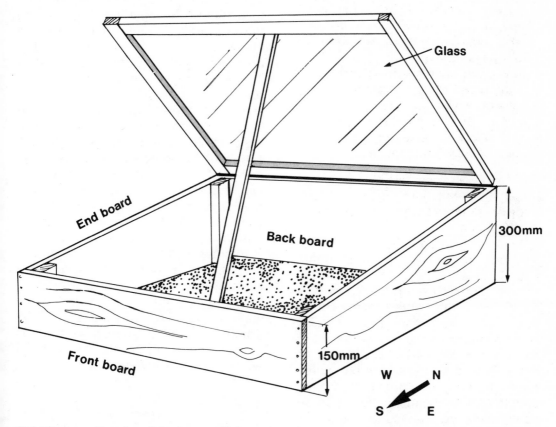

Cold frame   The size of the frame will depend on the number of seeds to be propagated. The frame should face south with protection from the north and east if possible

Propagation may be detailed as follows:

- In the frame, sow thinly in pots or boxes (placing the seeds 25 mm apart each way); plant outside into the final positions direct from the seed box or pot when the seedlings have two pairs of leaves.
- In the frame, sow thickly in pots or boxes, prick off into other boxes or pots in the frame, and plant outside when there are approximately four pairs of leaves.
- In the frame, sow thinly into the soil, placing the seeds 12 mm apart each way, or in rows 100 mm apart, and plant out when there are three or four pairs of leaves.
- Sow in an open seedbed and transplant when there are three or four pairs of leaves.
- Sow in situ and thin out if necessary.
- Sow thinly in boxes or pots in the open and then transplant.

The following general points about propagation will help in the success of the operation, as well as the planning of the garden.

By sowing in containers and transplanting, time on the main cropping area is gained. This can be illustrated by two general examples. Sowing in containers in the frame in early spring makes seed germinate more quickly than sowing outside, and while these plants are being raised more time is being allowed for the soil to be broken down. Sowing in containers in the open in summer means that while these plants are being raised, more time can be allowed for the crop(s) they are to replace. It also means that the frame space can be utilised in the summer once the glass has been taken off, the plants being raised on this area.

Sowing in containers gives the gardener much more control over the seedlings in respect of water, pests and diseases, especially when only 10 or 12 plants need to be raised. Often seedlings germinating in open ground are subject to soil capping; after rain the soil on the surface forms a skin, and if this dries out it becomes very hard on many soil types, and seedlings are unable to penetrate it. This either delays emergence of the seedlings or causes their death.

Seedlings should never be allowed to dry out while germinating—drying out after initial water uptake results in many propagation failures. Compost in containers should be completely soaked before sowing. After sowing has taken place, a covering of sieved compost should be added. Unless the seeds are large, e.g. peas or beans for which about a 25 mm covering is required, 6 mm of compost is adequate. There is no need to add further water, as capillary action will moisten the compost above the seeds. To avoid capping, watering should be avoided until after the emergence of the seedlings. If the containers do dry out before emergence, they should be stood in water until the surface is moist. To help keep the surface moist after sowing, polythene may be placed over the containers until the seedlings appear. As soon as they can be seen this must be removed or the seedlings will be drawn and thus spoilt.

too early for pricking out

correct stage for pricking out—
cotyledons fully expanded

too large for pricking out

If seedlings are to be pricked out, this should always be done at the 'cotyledon stage', as shown above, or as soon as they can be handled. The sooner they are pricked out, the less the check to the plant will be. It is most important that when you are pricking off seedlings, you should handle them all by the leaves only, never by the stems. Damage to the stems caused by handling leads to many losses.

A check in growth to the plants through being potbound or through starvation must be avoided. Planting out plants that have been checked in this way again causes many crop failures.

When plants have been raised in a frame they must always be hardened off before being planted out into the cropping area. If this is not done, wind in particular can cause scorching of leaves or plant losses. With vegetable plants this hardening-off process may be easily achieved by removing the glass from the frame for a few days before planting out or, if there are other plants that are not yet ready, removing the required plants (if they are in containers) and putting them in a sheltered position for a few days.

Checks caused by any of the above means may result in plants running to seed prematurely, or simply 'standing still'.

Seed is now much more expensive than it used to be, particularly that of hybrids, so sow only enough seed to produce the number of plants you needed. Normally 15%-20% more seeds should be sown than plants required, to allow for those which fail to germinate and those seedlings which are not up to standard and need rejecting. When planting or pricking out only those seedlings which look 'normal' should be used—the odd much larger or smaller seedling should be rejected as it may not be true to type, may already be affected by disease that cannot be seen easily or may simply be a weakling.

Planting

Depths of planting will vary depending on the type of crop. All plants must be planted firmly without damaging the stem. As previously noted, contact with the stem should be avoided when pricking out, and the same applies when planting out; the diagram below shows how this may be carried out. Loose planting will lead to the roots drying out before they have time to root out into the soil and wind will blow plants over or even out of the ground. Frost in the early part of the year will also lift plants out of the ground unless planting is firm.

When plants have been raised in peat pots, the bottom of the pot should be broken before planting to allow the roots to come into contact with the soil. It is quite possible for plants which have been raised in peat pots to die of lack of water even though the soil into which they have been planted is wet, because the peat pot prevents the roots taking up water from the soil. Plants raised in this way must always be soaked before planting so that the peat pot is thoroughly wet, and then the bottom of the pot must be broken open when planting takes place. Even with these precautions, if the weather is hot and sunny immediately after planting, the plant will use the water reserve in the peat pot before it can root into the soil and spot waterings may still be necessary a week after planting.

Planting with a dibber to avoid contact with the plant stem when planting out

wedge of soil between dibber and plant stem to prevent damage to stem when firming

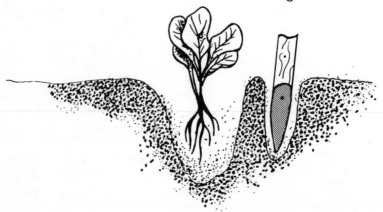

Use of Water

Water is becoming very precious, and the time when the amateur is most likely to need it is the very time when the Local Authority has been forced to impose restrictions. It is therefore most important to conserve water as much as possible. This can be achieved in the following ways:

■ Use a stale seed or planting bed if possible.
■ From May to September, keep a 25 mm dust mulch on the surface of the soil—this can even be done on ground being kept as a stale seed-bed. When it is planting or sowing time the mulch can be removed from the place where the seed is to be sown or the plant planted, see below.
■ If digging or forking is necessary during the summer, always break the soil down to a tilth and firm immediately. Avoid leaving soil in a loose condition.
■ Keep weeds hoed.

Using water can be thought of in two ways: to establish a crop and to alleviate drought. The establishment of crops can normally be done without any problem, the amount of water used being small. Even in the hottest weather plants firmly planted into a stale bed and given a pint of water each as they are planted rarely require further water. There are times when because of drought vegetable crops will benefit from irrigation if it is available. The timing of the application to gain maximum benefit may be of great importance and is discussed as each crop is described.

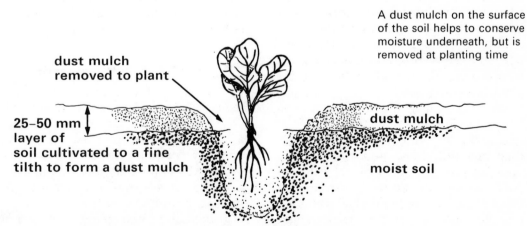

A dust mulch on the surface of the soil helps to conserve moisture underneath, but is removed at planting time

dust mulch removed to plant

25–50 mm layer of soil cultivated to a fine tilth to form a dust mulch

dust mulch

moist soil

soil beneath dust mulch is protected from drying out because it is insulated from sun and wind

Use of Chemicals

The use of chemicals in the garden is always a difficult subject.

If they are used it is most important to keep the concentrate away from children, preferably under lock and key. While it may be possible to grow ornamentals and possibly even fruit without using pesticides or fungicides, there are some vegetables for which chemicals must be used in order to obtain a crop. The following are examples where control with chemicals is often necessary: carrot fly and cabbage root fly; club root; bindweed; and creeping thistle. Chemicals should always be used with care and the manufacturers' instructions followed to the letter.

In general, spraying is best carried out in the evening when there is no wind, a reasonable temperature, and rain is not expected for six hours. Chemicals are an added expense and so should only be used when biological, cultural or 'handpicking' methods are not satisfactory. Spray drift must always be avoided, particularly when herbicides are being used.

Many chemicals are harmful to bees and other insects that are not pests. There are far more beneficial insects than harmful ones, and many carry out pollination, essential to fruit as well as vegetable crops, so destroying these must be avoided if at all possible. Equally important are the insects which parasitise the pests we are trying to kill. A certain pest level must be tolerated or the balance of nature will be upset.

It is advisable to have two sprayers, one for pesticides and fungicides, the other for herbicides. Using a sprayer for spraying a pesticide or fungicide after spraying a herbicide may result in disaster if there are traces of the herbicide left in the sprayer. Even if two sprayers are available, always wash out thoroughly after use. Always wear rubber gloves when using chemicals, and wash your hands as soon as you have finished.

When controls or preventative measures are described later, the active chemical rather than the proprietary name is quoted, so that there is no confusion. All chemicals sold should have the name of the active ingredient printed somewhere on the label. Always keep the label on a container. Never put a chemical into another type of container.

Biological and Cultural Control

Biological and cultural control have been mentioned in other contexts, but as far as amateurs are concerned, they are an important part of gardening, particularly when associated with vegetables. We eat vegetables almost every day of our lives—the less chemicals we have to put on the better.

If there are small yellow cocoons on brassica leaves near caterpillars leave well alone—it means the caterpillars are being parasitised by *apanteles glomeratus.* Ladybirds feed on aphids. Several small birds feed on insects. Starlings in particular feed on slugs, and everybody must have seen thrushes feeding on snails. Robins are very fond of cutworms, and so the list goes on—it is almost endless.

Cultural control for pests includes not only growing as much as possible when the pest is not active, but making sure rotations are strictly followed, and composting or burning the old crop debris. A build-up of any one particular disease may be prevented by taking the same precautions as for pests and, in addition, using resistant varieties, and avoiding damage to plants— botrytis in particular enters plants through a wound.

Pests, Diseases and Physiological Disorders

There are a vast number of pests, diseases and physiological disorders associated with vegetables, many of which are only problems in local areas. It is therefore not possible to describe each and every one, but the important issues are outlined in general here, while major problems of individual crops are discussed as the crops are described.

Always remember that prevention is the best cure; this can be achieved by bearing in mind the following:
- Maintain good hygiene—clear away empty seed boxes, old sticks, bricks and other rubbish.
- Keep to a disciplined rotation to prevent build-up of any pest or disease.
- Some crops can be grown early or late to avoid pests or diseases during the summer. An example is club root on cauliflower; the disease does not become really active until temperatures rise in the summer. If you have a deep freeze, therefore, and club root is a problem in your area, you can grow cauliflower early in the year (maturing in June or early July), harvest the crop before the disease is very active, and freeze it for use during the rest of the summer. An added advantage is that an early crop is normally also free of aphids and caterpillars because these too do not become fully active until later in the year.
- Never plant infected plants or plants that appear healthy but are known to have come from infected soil. This is one of the major ways in which diseases such as club root are spread. The point cannot be stressed strongly enough—it is difficult to refuse plants from friends and neighbours, but if there is any doubt don't plant. It may mean the difference between trouble-free crops and not being able to grow the crop at all in future.
- Allow biological control as much as possible. Spraying may upset the fine balance of nature, and a few pests must be tolerated or vegetables will 'taste of chemicals'.

Pests:

Aphids attack virtually all crops. There are many species, practically one for every crop, but many attack several crops. Besides sucking sap and distorting leaves, they leave honeydew which collects dirt and fungi, and some also transmit viruses. On a small scale, if plants are not hearted, hand-picking might be possible, but this is not always very practical and it may be that more damage is done by trying to pick them off than the aphids themselves are doing. A few aphids on a lettuce or cabbage when fully grown for the home kitchen are surely acceptable, as they can easily be washed off. The real damage is done in the seedling or half-grown stage—it is at this time that crops need to be sprayed. There are several chemical preparations to choose from that are effective. They usually contain one or more of the following: Malathion, Formothion, Resmethrin, B.H.C., and Derris.

Caterpillars are the larvae of many different kinds of moths and butterflies. As with the aphids, particular species feed only on a certain crop, but others attack a wide range of crops. Brassica crops are probably the worst affected. There are chemicals which can be used against caterpillars, but these are usually only effective for a short while and then only if the spray hits the caterpillar directly. The spraying must be done every 14 days from August to October but at the seedling and up to two-thirds grown stage, hand-picking the caterpillars is probably as effective as spraying. Apart from brassicas, other crops such as lettuce, sweet corn, spinach and almost any seedlings can be attacked by some moth larvae. Sprays used against them contain chemicals such as Formothion, Trichlophon, and Derris.

Eelworms are nearly all invisible to the naked eye. There are many different species, the potato eelworm causing the most obvious damage, but all live in the soil, and many are able to stay there without their host plants for years. Weeds can also act as hosts. There is no control available to the amateur, rotation being the most important preventative measure.

Mice are probably very much more of a problem than most people realise. They are the cause of many seeds failing to germinate, particularly peas and beans sown early, but if the problem is realised in time they are easy to control by trapping or using bait containing Warfarin or Coumatetralyl.

Pigeons, like rabbits, are particularly troublesome in certain districts, particularly those in or bordering rural areas. Apart from netting, thin wires on 1.75 m poles every metre across the garden will probably be as effective as anything. Gardeners have tried various methods of deterring pigeons for years, but the birds soon become used to the different scaring devices.

Rabbits can cause complete devastation in a couple of nights. The answer is netting, which is expensive, but in the areas where they are a problem there is no alternative unless you are in a position to trap or shoot. Even so, prevention is better than cure. See the diagram on p. 38.

Slugs can be dealt with easily with slug pellets containing Methiocarb or Metaldehyde, but the pellets must be put down the same day as planting or sowing to ensure prevention—after the slug has had its dinner is too late!

Sparrows will attack any young plants, particularly in spring. Black cotton 450 mm above the young plants tied to canes every 600 mm will usually protect crops. Netting, of course, will also help keep them off but is expensive. A good cat can be of value against these pests.

Wireworms are not usually troublesome in established vegetable gardens, but the beetle to which the larvae belong lays its eggs in grassland and so this pest may be a problem on new gardens which were previously grass. It's the sort of problem that is not discovered until the damage is done as they attack the roots of almost any crop when the grass which they normally feed on has been taken away.

Cultivation usually controls the pest eventually, but it may be checked by B.H.C.

Diseases:

Botrytis (or mould) will attack any plant. It usually enters the plant through a wound, which may have been caused by wind, pests, or bad handling by the gardener. There is now a control in the form of Benomyl, although some strains of botrytis are becoming resistant to the chemical.

Damping-off is a disease that is present in many soils and attacks seedlings in particular at and below ground level. It can be controlled by seed dressing containing the chemical Captan.

Physiological disorders may also be a problem. Just because a plant looks sick it does not necessarily have a pest or disease. There are many other reasons—the following list might help if there is no obvious pest or disease present: compaction; waterlogging; capping of the soil after sowing; F.Y.M. that is too fresh—this can form a toxic layer below the soil surface; too much fertiliser or too little; a trace element may be lacking; and even overcrowding. Many of these problems occur if basic cultivation is not carried out properly. The importance of this cannot be emphasised enough. Good cultivation takes you more than half-way to success.

Rabbit-proof fencing This may work out expensive but apart from trapping or shooting it is the only way to deter these pests

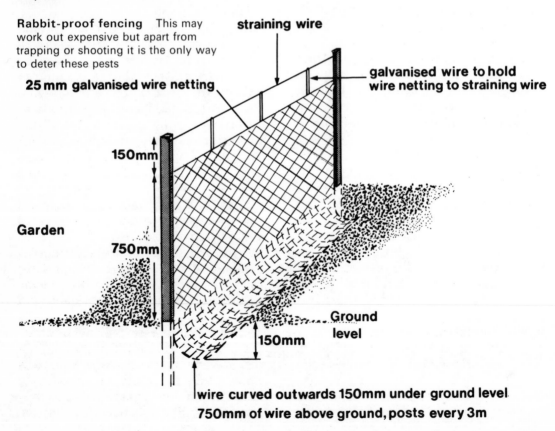

straining wire

galvanised wire to hold wire netting to straining wire

25 mm galvanised wire netting

150mm

Garden

750mm

Ground level

150mm

wire curved outwards 150mm under ground level
750mm of wire above ground, posts every 3m

Weed Control

The importance of weed control and how it may be achieved has in part already been mentioned under other headings, but because of its importance, no apology is made for repeating the points again. Weeds compete for nutrients, light and water; they are hosts to pests and diseases above and below ground, and perennial weed hinders cultivation. As with pests and diseases, prevention is better than cure. All annual weed can be controlled with hoeing or by hand; it is perennial weed which often presents a difficulty.

Weeds such as dock and dandelion can be dug out and put on the bonfire, and those such as bindweed and creeping thistle which are so difficult to dig out may be controlled by herbicides containing chemicals such as 2, 4, 5-T, and save many hours' work. There are a number of weedkillers available, some of which are selective and so do a particular job; but all should be used with caution and spray drift avoided—only spray on still evenings.

Hoeing of annual weed should be carried out when the weeds can hardly be seen, just as they are emerging; even seedlings of perennial weeds will be killed at this stage. This applies equally whether you are hoeing a stale bed or between crops. The final hoeing or raking of a stale bed should be immediately before sowing or planting so that the crop has a period with little or no weed. Some hand weeding along the rows of direct drilled crops such as carrot and beetroot is inevitable. This should be done as soon as the weed is big enough to handle.

It is doubtful if it is worth using selective weedkillers against annuals in crops because of their expense; also the success of the operation depends on several factors—correct soil moisture, correct temperature, correct stage of crop or weed growth, no wind to carry spray drift, no rain for a set number of hours after application, even coverage of area and correct rate.

Storage of Crops

It is very worthwhile being able to store carrots, parsnips, beetroot, onions, potatoes and marrows. All of these can be stored from harvesting in October, November and December through until February to May. Freezers are not dealt with in any detail, as storing vegetables in this way is adequately covered in other books. It is very doubtful if it is economical to store the above crops in a freezer if suitable storage space such as in a garage or cellar or old coal house is available. These places should be frost-free but also not subject to high temperature. The length of the storage will often depend on the weather conditions in March and April; if the weather turns very warm they will not keep so long.

Onions are stored dry. They can be hung up in old nylon stockings with a knot below each one so that they are isolated from each other, or in strings. Well-ripened marrows may also be stored dry until late January in open well-aired boxes.

Carrots, beetroot, and parsnips may all be stored in the same way in a box as the diagram below shows. It is important not to wash the vegetables before storage and only sound and undamaged roots should be stored. They can, of course, be put in a pie in

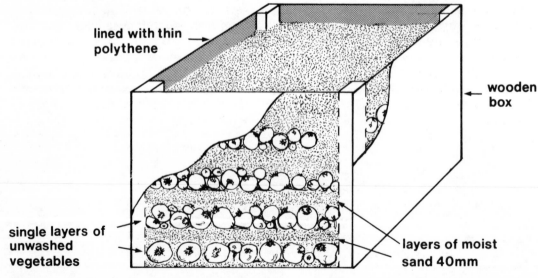

lined with thin polythene

wooden box

single layers of unwashed vegetables

layers of moist sand 40mm

A storage box like this is suitable for carrots, beetroot and parsnips. Place the box in a frost-free garage, cellar or shed.

A string of onions

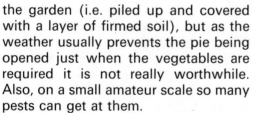

Place onions in an old nylon stocking,
knotting below each onion to separate them.
Cut below knot as required

the garden (i.e. piled up and covered
with a layer of firmed soil), but as the
weather usually prevents the pie being
opened just when the vegetables are
required it is not really worthwhile.
Also, on a small amateur scale so many
pests can get at them.

When harvesting carrots and parsnips, cut off the tops at the crown,
cut off the very long parsnip root, and
allow the vegetables to dry for a
couple of days before putting them
into store. Beetroot must be lifted
carefully, the tops screwed off by
hand and the tap root kept intact or
the roots will bleed while being
cooked.

Potatoes should also be allowed to
dry after lifting; they can then be
stored quite satisfactorily in hessian
or heavy duty paper bags.

Introduction to Crops and Varieties

Before describing the crops a few points on varieties and how to choose them should be made.

Choice of variety is very important. Virtually all seed catalogues give most excellent explanations of their varieties; this is done to help the gardener and those who ignore the advice may be courting disaster. It is not the aim of this book to describe every variety, and in any case new varieties are added every year, while others become unavailable. This makes it even more important that you should refer to your seedsmen's catalogues and choose the variety that suits your purpose best. What this book will try to do is to help you make that choice.

It is important not to try and make a variety do what it is not intended to do. For example, sowing summer cabbage in the autumn will only lead to disappointment—the variety to sow in the autumn is *spring* cabbage. In order that a crop may be grown all the year round, or as much of it as possible, several varieties may have to be bought. This puts up the expense but most seeds (except parsnips in particular) can be kept for at least two seasons, some for many more and so the cost may be spread over several years. Alternatively, a packet of seed can be shared between two or three people. By this means the final cost will often be only a few pence, even if you use hybrid seed, which is always more expensive because pollination to pro-

duce the seed has to be controlled. Known parents give a known result but seed from these hybrids cannot be kept because the resulting seedlings will revert back to the parents and other lines.

Although hybrid seed is initially more expensive it has several advantages which in the long run might make it more economical. The plants are more uniform and therefore mature more or less together; this enables quicker turn-round of crops, and may allow two crops per year on a given area rather than only one, thus helping those who own deep freezes. It also helps in producing a succession, particularly if you are able to discipline yourself to sow in succession and only plant the required number each time.

Knowing how long a crop takes to mature can save the embarrassment of having all the vegetables ready to harvest while you are away on holiday. By working back from the expected maturity date, a sowing date can be arrived at to avoid producing vegetables when they are not required. Extremes of weather will unfortunately sometimes upset such a plan.

Choice may be influenced by size. This will depend on your family; a family of two, for example, will only require a small type of lettuce while one of six might need a large plant.

Day-length is an important consideration as far as some crops are concerned. Short day varieties will run straight to seed if grown in high summer, but summer varieties will probably not be hardy enough to grow in winter; many varieties are not winter hardy, so it is no good trying to overwinter them.

The choice may be influenced by storage qualities; some varieties will keep considerably better and longer than others. For many crops there are varieties specially bred for deep freezing. Another important aspect to consider is speed to maturity, particularly if two crops are hoped for in one year off the same area of soil. By and large, paradoxical as it may sound, if late crops are required from a late sowing early varieties should be used, as they are normally quicker maturing. While some varieties may be grown all the year round, indeed some are called 'All the Year Round', they normally perform best at a certain season and other varieties are better for other seasons. Lastly, location of site may influence choice, particularly in northern areas. It has already been mentioned that early varieties mature more quickly. Because the growing season is normally shorter in the north, early varieties may be the only ones that are able to mature, a good example of this being sweetcorn.

Saving seed from your crops is not advised unless some experience has been acquired. With a few crops, for example runner beans, the process is not too difficult, but if you are producing vegetables for the kitchen, the length of time necessary to select the correct plants for producing seed, clean the seed, and dry and store it properly, makes it doubtful whether the whole operation is worthwhile, not to mention the fact that the seed plants will be taking up space that could be used for cropping.

The length of season over which any particular vegetable is available very much depends on temperatures in early spring and late autumn, apart from such crops as cabbage, for example, which, using several varieties, may be hearted all the year round, or crops such as sweetcorn that can only be matured in late summer or early autumn.

Spacing of Vegetables

Much research work has been carried out to find the optimum spacings for vegetables. Given the correct length of growing season, the optimum spacing may not necessarily produce the size of crop that an amateur requires; but having said this, within extremes of very large and very small, the yield per square metre of any crop in terms of weight will not vary greatly however many plants there are in that square metre. For example, 35 carrots per square metre will probably produce the same weight as 55 per square metre—the individual size of the carrots will of course be bigger if the number per square metre is less.

There are other considerations too. Close spacing has the effect of maturing many crops more quickly, wider spacing that of delaying maturity. But with large-seeded crops such as beans and peas, for which the seed is so costly, money can be saved by making sure that each plant is given sufficient space to yield fully, thus reducing the number of seeds needed. For example, peas sown at about 150 seeds per square metre will yield the same crop as 300 seeds per square metre—the plants at the lower seed rate are able to produce more pods per plant because they have the space.

These effects on spacing can be put to good use. If there are only two in your family, you can take advantage of the fact that closer spacing will produce smaller plants. You may only want a small cabbage each time, so they may be planted at a closer spacing than the norm—for a larger family of six, say, a wider spacing is necessary, to produce a larger plant.

However, to obtain maximum yield with some crops such as radishes and carrots, the seed needs to be sown broadcast very thinly giving each plant equal area, but this makes weeding difficult unless a stale seed-bed is used so that most weeds have been eradicated before sowing. The spacing of a crop, therefore, might be governed partly by the need to leave enough space between plants for cultivation while they are growing.

A Selection of Vegetables to Grow in the Open

In order to make reference easy, each crop is detailed and discussed in the following manner.

 Season of crop and if a succession is possible.

 (a) B.O.M. (including F.Y.M.) or compost requirement (to be dug in previously).
(b) Fertiliser requirement as a base dressing (to be applied when the soil is being broken down to a tilth).
(c) Fertiliser requirement as a top dressing (to be applied to the soil around the plants as they are growing).

It is important that fertiliser is not allowed to lodge in the leaves as it will cause scorching and may even kill the growing point.

The B.O.M. (or compost) and fertiliser rates given are for normal average soil conditions and may need to be adjusted according to experience of the soil in any particular garden.

 Details of sowing and planting, including the spacing required. Where instructions such as 'sow in March-April' are given, you must decide when the right moment is by considering such matters as geographical location, weather and soil conditions.

 Expected yield from a given area.

 Particular pests and diseases.

 When to irrigate if there is a drought.

 Special notes, if any.

Brassica Group

The Brassica Crop

Besides the general pests mentioned previously, all brassica crops suffer particularly from two problems restricted to them: club root and cabbage root fly. **Club root** is a soil-borne disease and particularly difficult to eradicate once established. Calomel dust can be used and will ensure a crop, but it is expensive. To help avoid the effects of club root, it is important to ensure that the pH of the soil is kept at 7–7.5.

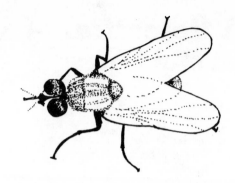

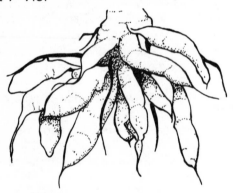

The **cabbage root fly** lays its eggs in the soil surface and the maggots burrow into the roots, killing them and so causing the plant's death or reducing the yield drastically. This can be controlled by placing granules containing Diazinon around the base of the plant immediately after planting.

Rotation is an important factor in helping to prevent either of these two problems, particularly club root.

All the brassicas mentioned will freeze well but it must be left up to the individual to decide the economics of this. Remember brassicas can be grown throughout the year; but it may be easier to grow a particular crop (as mentioned previously when discussing hybrid seed), harvest it all on the same day, and freeze that which is not required, thus leaving the land immediately available for another crop. In northern areas in particular, a factor which may be worth considering is that in this way you can avoid having to harvest during severe weather in winter. Another advantage of growing an early crop is that caterpillars and other pests and diseases may be avoided.

Brassicas in particular respond to spacing. The spacings which follow are for producing average sizes, but if you require larger or smaller heads of cabbage or cauliflower, or prefer bigger or smaller sprouts, the plants should be spaced farther apart or closer together accordingly.

Brassicas must always be planted firmly and up to the base of the growing point.

Brussels Sprouts

 The season can be from August right through until the following March but most people only require them from October to February. Brussels sprouts are very hardy and will withstand the hardest weather.

 (a) Dig in F.Y.M. or compost up to 20 kg per sq m.
(b) Apply 85 g per sq m of general compound fertiliser plus 50 g per sq m of N-only fertiliser.
(c) Top dress in July or August around the plants with N-only fertiliser at the rate of 35 g per sq m.

 Most gardeners will want two varieties, one to mature mid-season and one for later on.
(a) Sow in the frame in March, remove the glass as soon as the second leaves appear and transplant in April-May.
(b) Sow outside in March-April in a seedbed (not in pots) and then transplant in May-June 600 mm apart each way.

 Sprouts are picked off the stem from the bottom up as they mature and so yield is not easy to estimate; however, each plant should yield about 1.8 kg. 16–20 plants are normally enough for the average family. If the plant tops are picked before they run to seed in the New Year, they may be cooked and eaten like cabbage.

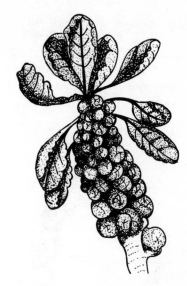

 Pests and diseases are as already described.

 Irrigation is not usually necessary.

 When picking the sprouts, don't remove the leaves from the ones that are not yet mature and are being left to grow on. Removing the tops of the plants before November will make the sprouts mature all together and advance the maturity date.

Cabbages

 Cabbage is the easiest crop of all to achieve fresh all the year round, the winter types being very hardy.

 (a) Dig in B.O.M. or compost up to 20 kg per sq m.
(b) For all except spring cabbage, which is planted in the autumn for overwintering, apply 85 g per sq m of general

compound fertiliser plus 50 g per sq m of N-only fertiliser.

(c) Top dress spring cabbage only, when growth begins in the new year, with 35 g per sq m of N-only fertiliser.

 Sowings to achieve a succession may be detailed as follows:

Early summer cabbage: Sow in the frame in February-March, prick off and grow on in the frame before planting in April-May. It will be ready to cut June-July.

Summer cabbage: Sow outside in March-May, planting in May-June, or alternatively sow direct in drills and thin when the seedlings are large enough to handle. The plants will mature in July-September.

Autumn cabbage: Sow outside in May, planting in June or alternatively sow direct in drills and thin when the seedlings are large enough. Autumn cabbage matures in October-December.

Winter cabbage: Sow outside in May and plant in June-July or alternatively sow direct in drills and thin later. The plants will mature December-March.

Spring cabbage: Sow outside in July-August and plant in August-September or alternatively sow direct in drills in August-September and thin later. The cabbage will be ready to cut in March-June. If you are planting spring cabbage, as opposed to sowing direct, the extra time is needed for the plants to establish themselves before the colder autumn days set in.

Planting distances are 600 mm between rows and 375 mm between plants for summer, autumn and winter cabbage; 300 mm between rows and 225 mm between plants for spring cabbage. Winter and spring cabbage are best sown in a seedbed outside (not in pots) and then transplanted.

 Yield: You will get one head (1–1.5 kg) of summer, autumn, or winter cabbage per 0.25 sq m. Spring cabbage, if allowed to heart (but it can be cut before), will give approximately 7.25 kg per sq m.

 Pests and diseases are as already described. As with cauliflowers, the overwintered spring cabbage and early summer cabbage tend to avoid the major problems.

 Irrigation is beneficial until the hearts have become hard.

 If they are checked by cold in the spring, the early summer round-headed varieties are likely to run to seed.

Calabrese

A variety of broccoli, this is one of the newer vegetables and will probably be unfamiliar to most people. It is not difficult to grow but is very pleasant to eat, giving a change from cauliflower or cabbage. Calabrese is excellent for freezing.

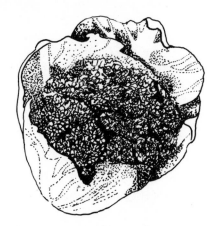

 Once the main head has been removed the side shoots can be left to develop later; the season is July-December.

 (a) Dig in F.Y.M. or compost up to 20 kg per sq m.
(b) Apply 85 g per sq m of general compound fertiliser plus 35 g per sq m of N-only fertiliser.
(c) No top dressing is required.

 Sow direct April-June in rows 600 mm apart and thin when big enough to 300 mm between the plants. Calabrese does not like being transplanted. The vegetable matures from July until the end of the year.

 The yield is approximately 0.7 kg per plant.

 Pests and diseases are as already described.

 Irrigation will increase the yield. Water when the curds are first forming.

Cauliflower and Broccoli

 Taking the two vegetables together, a succession can be obtained from March through to December in most areas in most years. The months from March to June are covered by broccoli that has overwintered, and from June to December cauliflower is available. The curds of cauliflower are not completely frost-hardy, but in favoured areas or during mild winters curds may be cut every month of the year.

 (a) Dig in B.O.M. or compost up to 20 kg per sq m.
(b) Apply 85 g per sq m of general compound fertiliser plus 50 g per sq m of N-only fertiliser.
(c) When growth starts in the

new year, broccoli should be top dressed around the plants with N-only fertiliser at the rate of 35 g per sq m. Cauliflower should not require a top dressing.

 Sowings to achieve succession may be detailed as follows, using the correct varieties for the particular seasons:

(a) Sow cauliflower in late September-early October in the frame, prick off into 90 mm pots, using sterilised potting compost, and leave in the frame until February-March. Harden off and plant out —the plants will mature in May-June.

(b) Sow cauliflower in February-April in the frame, prick out and grow on in the frame until the plants are ready for planting in April-May. The cauliflower will mature in July-August.

(c) Sow cauliflower in the open in April-May for planting in May-June. The plants will mature in the autumn.

(d) Sow broccoli in the open in April-May for planting in June and overwintering. It will mature the following year in March-June, according to the severity of winter and the variety of broccoli grown.

Planting distances are: cauliflower—600 mm between the rows, 450 mm between the plants; broccoli—600 mm each way. Broccoli is best sown in a seedbed outside (not in pots) and then transplanted.

 Yield: One cauliflower per 0.25 sq m; one broccoli per 0.35 sq m.

 Pests and diseases are as already described. Remember early summer cauliflower largely avoids all the problems.

 Irrigation is most beneficial if applied just as the curd is forming (about 15 mm in diameter). This will normally apply to summer cauliflower.

 To do well, cauliflower needs to be kept growing all the time without a check. The plants are also quickly affected by the weather, which may delay or advance them according to temperature. Broccoli is more tolerant but may die in severe winters.

Purple Sprouting

This vegetable, a variety of broccoli, is not often seen in the shops because it wilts quickly and must be cooked the same day as it is harvested. It is not difficult to grow and makes a delicious change from the normal run of vegetables.

 This is a very hardy crop and yields very prolifically. The season is February-April. As with calabrese, once the main shoot has been cut (and sometimes before this) the plant throws out a profusion of secondary shoots.

 (a) Dig in F.Y.M. or compost up to 20 kg per sq m.
(b) Apply 85 g per sq m of general compound fertiliser plus 35 g per sq m of N-only fertiliser.

(c) Top dressing may be applied in the new year at the rate of 35 g per sq m of N-only fertiliser.

 Sow in a seedbed outside in May, and transplant in June with 600 mm between the seedlings each way. The plants mature the following February-April.

 The yield is difficult to estimate but 6–10 plants will provide enough for the average family.

 Pests and diseases are as already described.

 Irrigation is not usually required.

Radishes

The quickest-maturing of all vegetables, and one of the easiest, radishes take up

very little room and can be grown between other, slower-growing vegetables.

 In the summer the small varieties will mature in 28 days. A succes-

sion can be grown throughout the summer but after early July they very quickly become 'woody' because of the warmer weather and run to seed. They are at their best in late spring and early summer.

 (a) No B.O.M. or compost is required.
(b) Apply 85 g per sq m of general compound fertiliser.
(c) No top dressing is necessary.

 Sow 18 seeds per 300 mm, with 100 mm between rows. There is no need to thin. For a succession throughout the summer, repeat the sowing every 2 weeks from March to June.

 2 bunches per 300 mm of row.

 Flea beetles sometimes attack the seedlings. Spraying is rarely worthwhile as the crop grows quickly enough to outpace them, if aided by irrigation in dry weather.

 Irrigation in dry weather is essential during the growing period.

 Remember radishes are a member of the brassica family and in summer can be attacked by club root, so rotation is important if they are to be grown throughout the summer months. Rotation for the early sowing is not so important. Radishes can usefully be intercropped if they are sown at the same time as, or up to 14 days later than, beetroot for example. The radishes will mature before they are competing for space with the beetroot crop.

Legume Group

Broad Beans

Broad beans are excellent for freezing.

 This is a hardy crop but one sowing of the same variety will tend to mature all at once. The season is only fairly short, June-August.

 (a) No B.O.M. or compost is required.
(b) Apply 85 g per sq m of general compound fertiliser only.
(c) No top dressing is necessary.

 There are two sowing times: October or November for over-wintering, using the correct variety, or from March to early May. Sow 50 mm deep in rows 600 mm apart, with 150 mm between seeds.

 The yield (of beans in the pods) is approximately 3 kg per m run.

 Bean weevil is sometimes a problem and it can be controlled with a spray containing B.H.C.

 Irrigation is not necessary.

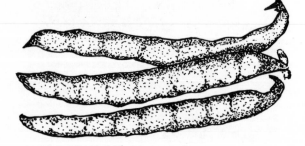

 This crop depends on bees pollinating the flowers, and it is therefore not possible to advance the crop. Poor weather at flowering time will result in poor yields.

French Beans

This crop takes a shorter time to reach maturity than runner beans, and many people prefer them anyway because they are stringless. French beans are also a good crop for freezing.

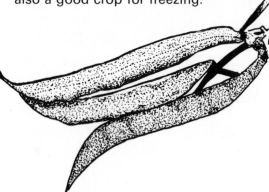

 The crop is susceptible to frost, so the season is late June/July-October.

 (a) B.O.M. or compost is not necessary, but French beans enjoy a rich soil.
(b) Apply 85 g per sq m of general compound fertiliser.
(c) Top dressing is not necessary.

 For the earliest crops sow in pots —two or three seeds per pot— in the frame in early May. Plant out when the danger of frost has passed in rows 450 mm apart, 150 mm between plants. Main crops are sown in the open in drills 40-50 mm deep during May, 20 seeds per m run, 450 mm between rows. A late crop to mature in late September/October may be sown in the first week of July.

 The beans are picked as they are large enough. The crop will yield approximately 1.5 kg per m run in total.

 There are no particular pests or diseases.

 Irrigation is beneficial during periods of drought.

 Cold weather can have a particularly detrimental effect on this crop during the early stages. The seed will germinate badly if the weather remains cold and wet after sowing. There are several types, some climbing, but most gardeners grow the dwarf variety.

Peas

Many varieties are excellent for freezing, provided they are harvested when young.

 The pea crop is not susceptible to frost but because of the temperatures required for flowering the crop's season is from June-October. A succession is fairly easy to accomplish throughout this time.

 (a) No B.O.M. or compost should be dug in.
(b) Apply 85 g per sq m of general compound fertiliser.

Three methods of staking peas

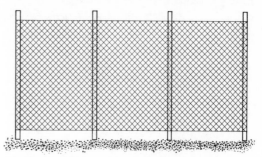

Netting held in position with canes

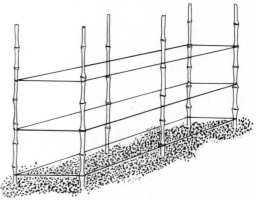

Canes 1–1½ m high with string every 150–225 mm

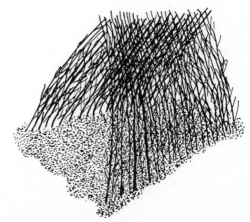

Birch brush wood 1 m high—very effective but not always easy to obtain

(c) No top dressing is necessary.

 Sow 40–50 mm deep from March to June in a succession if desired. It is necessary to stake this crop. As seen, the method of sowing will depend on the staking. Early varieties should be sown more thickly than later varieties; sow peas 50–65 per m in drills, 40–50 mm apart in bands. If you are sowing in late June, use an early variety.

 Yield is approximately 1.5 kg per m run for early varieties, unpodded, and 2.25–3 kg per m run of main crop tall varieties (double runs).

 Pea moth is a pest on the midsummer crops. Use a spray containing Trichlorphon just as the pods are forming.

 Irrigation should only be applied just as the main pods are beginning to swell or too much leaf and haulm will be made.

Runner Beans

This is another crop which freezes well.

 The season is from late July until the first frost in the autumn. Like French beans, runner beans are susceptible to frost.

 (a) Dig in F.Y.M. or compost up to 20 kg per sq m.
(b) Apply 85 g per sq m of general compound fertiliser plus 15 g per sq m of N-only fertiliser.
(c) There is no need to top dress.

 For the earliest crops sow in pots, one seed per pot, in the frame during May, planting out after the chance of frost has passed. Alternatively, sow direct in late May. This crop needs staking as 1.75–2.5 m in height is required; for staking methods see opposite. When planting, put 1 or 2 plants at the base of each support; when sowing, put three seeds at the base of each.

 Yield: Approximately 2.25 kg per support.

 There are no particular pests or diseases.

 Irrigation is important during dry weather and yields are greatly increased if it can be given.

 This crop does best if the weather is warm, provided water is available. It also relies on bees, particularly bumble bees, to pollinate the flowers—no crop will be achieved if the flowers are not pollinated. Runner beans may also be grown as a bush, rather than trained up sticks. The yield is not so heavy but the beans come as much as 14 days earlier, and being low on the ground are less liable to wind damage on exposed sites. Pinching out the growing points has the effect of making the plant produce flower trusses earlier, besides forming the plant into a bush. The pinching needs to be done at least once a week for eight weeks; see below. Short-podded varieties should be used as there is less likelihood of the pods trailing on the ground.

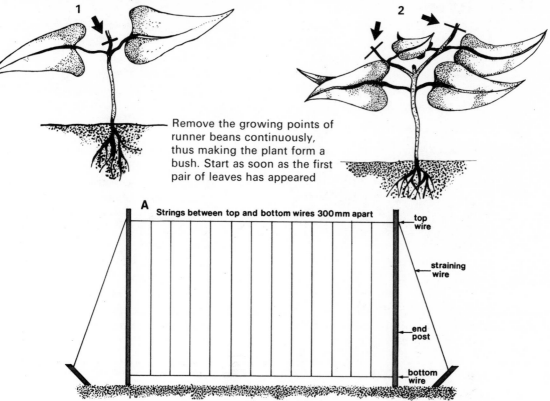

Remove the growing points of runner beans continuously, thus making the plant form a bush. Start as soon as the first pair of leaves has appeared

A Strings between top and bottom wires 300 mm apart

top wire

straining wire

end post

bottom wire

Two methods of staking runner beans; (**A**) may be used for a single or double row; while (**B**) shows a tented double row. A third method, not shown, is to tie four canes together at the top to form a wigwam. The canes should be set 750 mm apart at the bottom, and there should be 900 mm between wigwams

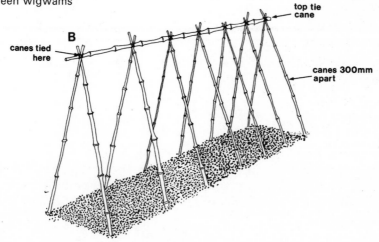

top tie cane

canes tied here

B

canes 300mm apart

Onion Group

Bulb Onions

 A succession can be obtained virtually all year round with storage, particularly with the recent introduction of early-maturing Japanese onions.

 (a) Dig in B.O.M. or compost up to 20 kg per sq m.
(b) Apply 85 g per sq m of general compound fertiliser plus 50 g per sq m of N-only fertiliser (even for the Japanese onions that are sown in the autumn).
(c) Autumn-sown crops should be top dressed with N fertiliser only, 35 g per sq m when growth begins in the new year. Main crop onions will benefit from a top dressing in July (June for onion sets) of N fertiliser only, 35 g per sq m.

 To produce the main crop for autumn use and storing until the following April, alternatives are as follows:
(a) Plant sets in January-March, with 300 mm between rows, 150 mm between sets.
(b) Sow seed in the frame in January-February, prick off, grow on in the frame, and plant out in April-May, 100-150 mm apart, 300 mm between rows.
(c) Sow seed thinly in containers in the frame in January-February, leaving 15 mm space each way, and plant out in April 100–150 mm apart, with 300 mm between rows.

(d) Sow direct in the open in March, 40 seeds per m, 300 mm between rows.

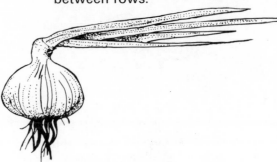

For onions to use in May-July the timing of the sowing is critical, to ensure that the onions overwinter satisfactorily. Sowings should be made in August in the north, September in the south; the extremes of the countrywide sowing period are approximately 14th August and 14th September. Sow in rows 300 mm apart, 40 seeds per m run.

 The yield will be 1.5–3 kg per m run.

 Provided rotation is properly adhered to, pests and diseases should not build up. White rot can be prevented by using calomel. Onion fly may also cause some problems but not usually in sufficient quantities to justify expensive control, though Diazinon granules applied before the fly attacks in areas where it is known to be a problem will give control.

 The crop will survive without irrigation but if there is a drought during June and July the yield can be increased by watering.

Onions from sets usually mature and ripen off from August onwards without problems. Maincrop onions from seed should be bent over at the neck in late August-early September to stop them from growing; they should be lifted in late September-early October and when dry taken into store. Japanese onions need the above treatment in late May-July according to variety, but they are not meant for winter storing. Only grow enough to use between May and September. The winters have been mild since these onions were introduced and they have yet to prove themselves during a severe winter.

Leeks

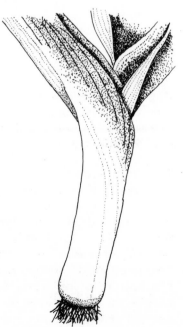

Leeks are an easy crop to grow and provide valuable fresh vegetables during winter and early spring.

 Leeks can be cropped from early autumn, but most people do not require them until January-April. They have a long growing season.

 (a) Dig in B.O.M. or compost up to 20 kg per sq m.
(b) Apply 85 g per sq m of general compound fertiliser plus 35 g per sq m of N-only fertiliser.
(c) Top dressing is not usually necessary.

 Sow 100 seeds per m run in the frame, preferably into the soil, in February-March, taking the glass off in April. Plant out in June with 100-150 mm between plants, 300 mm between rows. Alternatively, sow direct in the open in March-April, 35 seeds per m run, 300 mm between rows, and thin the young seedlings to 100-150 mm apart.

 Yield: 2.25-3 kg per m run (this rather depends on how severely the leeks are trimmed. Some people prefer more green than others.)

 There are no particular pests or diseases.

 Irrigation is not usually necessary.

 In order to obtain a greater length of white stem, leeks can be earthed up; if you wish to do this, you must leave 600 mm between the rows for access.

Salad Onions

 A succession of salad onions may be achieved very nearly all the year round, severe weather in winter being the only limiting factor. The plants are quite frost-hardy but the tops will need to regrow after a spell of severe winter weather before the onions can be eaten.

 (a) Dig in F.Y.M. or compost up to 20 kg per sq m.
(b) Apply 85 g per sq m of general compound fertiliser plus 35 g per sq m of N-only fertiliser. Leave out the N-only fertiliser for overwintering crops.
(c) Top dress overwintering crops only in February/March with N fertiliser only, at a rate of 35 g per sq m.

 A succession may be achieved by sowing the onion seed from July until October for over-wintering and starting to sow again in March, continuing to sow about once per month until June. Sow 35 seeds per 300 mm, leaving 225–300 mm between rows.

 You will be able to pick four good bunches per 300 mm of a single row.

 Onion fly usually attacks in the height of the summer but normally only a few of the plants are affected and it is doubtful if it is worth carrying out any control measures. However, for the crops sown in April and

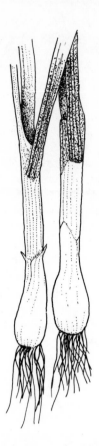

May a dressing containing Diazinon can be applied to the seed-bed before sowing.

 Irrigation is not usually necessary but it will improve the yield in drought conditions while the crop is growing.

 The onions from each sowing can be used over quite a long period of time. So only short rows are required at any one time unless your family has a passion for onions! It is probably best to set aside one or two rows across the plot and sow a section of row four or five times throughout the year.

`Others' Group

Herbs

All cooks know the difference fresh herbs can make to a dish, and they need take up very little room. Of the six most widely-used herbs, rosemary and bay are shrubs but parsley, thyme, chives and sage can easily be grown from seed.

 Bay is a long-lived shrub, but may be killed by a severe winter, so in northern areas it may be advisable to grow it in a large pot so that it can be moved and given protection from the worst weather. Rosemary (also a shrub) is not very long-lived, but will last longer than the two or three years which the other four herbs mentioned should be allowed. Chives and sage will be available for use all year round, but thyme and parsley may die back in severe winters.

 (a) B.O.M. or compost is not essential.
(b) Apply 85 g per sq m of compound fertiliser.
(c) Top dressing of compound fertiliser should be applied in February after overwintering, at the rate of 50 g per sq m.

 There is room for all six herbs on a patch of land 6 m × 1 m, of which rosemary and bay require 1 sq m each.
Rosemary and bay are normally bought as young plants. Bay is not easy to propagate but rose-

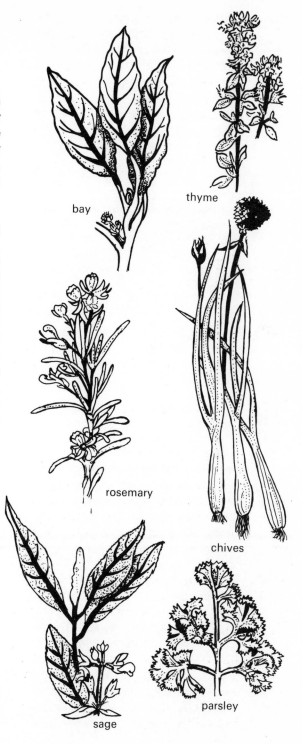

bay

thyme

rosemary

chives

sage

parsley

mary, once obtained, can be propagated from cuttings in the frame in June or July. The 100 mm cuttings should be inserted in a pot of compost consisting of half peat and half sand, placed in the frame, covered with a sheet of glass or polythene and shaded until rooted, when the shading and glass are removed for hardening off before winter.

Parsley, thyme, chives and sage are easily grown from seed sown in drills during April. The rows should be 300 mm apart, and the plants thinned to 200 mm apart.

 One shrub each of rosemary and bay and one patch 1 m square of each of the others will normally yield sufficient for the average family.

 There are no particular pests or diseases.

 Some irrigation may be necessary for the parsley to keep it fresh but the others are more drought-resistant. If the bay is in a pot it should be watered regularly and never allowed to dry out in the summer.

 To keep rosemary productive it should be cut back in May so that it forms a tight bush. This may need to be repeated later in the year. Only the leaves of bay are required but the shrub will stand clipping in the summer and can be grown into a formal shape. Because bay and rosemary live longer than the other four herbs, it may be better to plant these two in a corner on their own or in the shrub border, so that they do not interfere with rotation. The other herbs produce better quality growth if renewed every two years and therefore will normally fit into a rotation.

Marrows and Courgettes

Marrows have long been a favourite with gardeners, and courgettes are rapidly growing in popularity.

 The cultivation of these two crops is very similar, the main difference being the size the vegetables are allowed to attain. Marrows may weigh a few kilos before being cut, but the average courgette should weigh approximately 110 g. Marrows therefore take much longer to reach maturity. The plants are not hardy, so the season lasts from July until the first frost, though well-ripened marrows may be stored until January provided they are harvested before the first frost.

 (a) Dig in B.O.M. or compost, up to 20 kg per sq m.
(b) Apply 85 g per sq m of basic compound fertiliser plus 35 g per sq m of N-only fertiliser.
(c) No top dressing is required.

Sow in the frame in pots, two seeds per pot, in the second week in May; discard the weaker seedling and plant out when the danger of frost is over. Alternatively, sow outside between the last week of May and mid-June. Allow 0.8 sq m for each plant. When sowing outside, sow three seeds together and thin to one plant when the cotyledons are expanded.

 In a small garden bush varieties are much easier to manage than

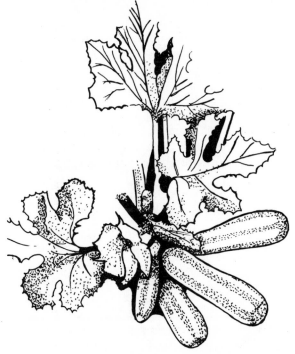

trailing varieties and although the fruits are smaller, more are produced per plant. Provided the summer weather is reasonable, a bush marrow will produce a marrow every 10 days if the fruits are not allowed to ripen— if they are left, the plant will allow all the nutrients to go into

the one fruit until this has matured. Courgettes must also be cut regularly to obtain high yield, about twice a week—as soon as the fruits reach the size of a sausage. Again, if the fruits are allowed to grow larger only one or two will be produced until they have ripened. If marrows are required ripe or for storage it is better to have separate plants from those used for summer cutting. After planting, simply leave them and harvest at the end of the season. Most plants will produce about four ripe marrows each.

 Virus can be a problem. As soon as you see the symptoms, which first appear in the growing point —this becomes pale in colour and distorted—pull the plant up to avoid spreading the virus to other plants. There is no control.

 Marrows benefit from irrigation particularly as the fruits are swelling. Courgettes benefit throughout their growing season.

 With both crops, at least two plants should always be grown to ensure pollination. It should not be necessary to have to pollinate by hand. It is most important that the plants do not receive a check from any cause when in pots in the frame—they never seem to recover properly from this, so if you are in any doubt as to whether it is too cold to sow your marrows, wait a while longer.

Spinach

If you like spinach, you will know how much better it is if cooked when fresh. Because it wilts very quickly, it is rarely seen in shops, and is a particularly rewarding crop to grow.

 This is one of the crops that is cut and grows again to be recut. It is not a difficult crop to grow and some varieties last right through the winter.

 (a) No B.O.M. or compost is required.
(b) Apply 85 g per sq m of general compound fertiliser.
(c) Top dressing is not necessary.

 Sow 8–10 seeds per 300 mm in April-May, thinning to 200–225 mm apart.

 Once it is established, a row 6 m long will provide enough during the growing season for the average family, if it is cut every 10–14 days.

 There are no particular pests or diseases.

 This is a leafy crop and in dry spells irrigation is worthwhile.

 To keep the leaves young, cutting must be reasonably frequent.

Sweetcorn

This crop is better suited for climatic reasons to the southern half of the country but is is possible to grow it in the north, though yields will be lighter. Sweetcorn is growing in popularity in this country, and is excellent for freezing.

 Sweetcorn is susceptible to more than 1° or 2°C of frost— and wind. The cobs ripen in late August-September, depending on the district and weather. The crop will tend to mature all together, though this is no problem if you have a freezer.

 (a) B.O.M. or compost is not essential.
(b) Apply 85 g per sq m of general compound fertiliser.
(c) Top dressing is not required.

 Sowings may take place as follows depending on geographical location:
Northern areas: Sow one seed per pot in late April in the frame, and plant out when the danger of frost has passed with 600 mm between rows, 375 mm between plants. Use an early variety.
Midland areas: Sow the early variety in mid-May in the open with 600 mm between rows,

375 mm between plants. Sow three seeds per station (i.e. together), thinning to one when the plants are 75–100 mm high. Sow the maincrop variety in April in pots in the frame, one seed per pot, and plant out as above a month later.

Southern areas: A longer season of cropping is possible here, with the early varieties maturing in summer and maincrop varieties following on. To achieve a good succession the early varieties can be sown in the frame from the end of March and planted out as above and the maincrop variety sown direct in mid-May as above.

 Yields vary considerably depending on location and the weather, but in the north one cob per plant can be expected, in the Midlands one cob for early varieties and one or two for maincrop, and in the south one or two cobs for early varieties and two for the maincrop variety.

 There are no particular pests or diseases.

 Irrigation is not important.

 This crop does much better in a warm summer, because it needs a fairly high temperature to grow well, and sun to ripen the cobs properly. Because the crop is adversely affected by wind, try to grow it in a sheltered position. Pollination, which is by wind and not by insects, is very important, and it is therefore essential to plant the crop in a square block and not in single rows. To ensure pollination it is advisable to shake the male flower onto the female at the flowering time. To get the best out of your crop, it is important to harvest it at the right time. The cobs should be picked just as the kernels are turning a pale butter yellow. The kernels should be milky and succulent—don't wait too long or they become flowery and dry to eat.

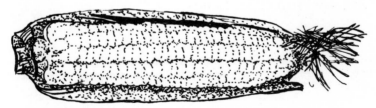

Potatoes

If you have enough space available for storage, which is simple with this crop, it is not difficult to provide potatoes for consumption all year round. At one time it was doubtful whether it was economically worth growing maincrop potatoes, but this may no longer be the case, and potatoes may be an additionally attractive proposition if they fit in with the planning of your rotation.

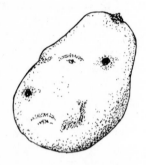

 Apart from the most favoured areas in the south and west, the earliest potatoes can be lifted in June, the succession continuing from then until October. The crop is susceptible to frost and you must make sure that frost damage is avoided on the growing foliage and on mature tubers.

 (a) Dig in B.O.M. or compost up to 20 kg per sq m.
(b) Apply 85 g per sq m of basic compound fertiliser plus 50 g per sq m of N-only fertiliser.
(c) Top dressing may be given at the rate of 35 g per sq m of N-only just before the foliage touches between the rows.

 Plant 75 mm deep as follows:
Early crops: Plant in February in the south and west, March in the north, with 450 mm between rows and 200–230 mm between tubers.
Main crops: Plant in mid-April with 675 mm between rows and 250–300 mm between tubers.

 It is not worth lifting early potatoes until they are the size of hens' eggs, approximately 450–675 g per tuber. In autumn, when the main crop is mature, a 50 g tuber should yield approximately 1 kg. Allowing for failures, 3 kg of seed potatoes should yield approximately 45 kg.

 Although stem eelworms have been mentioned in general previously, the importance of potato root eelworm must be stressed. Once established in the soil it is very difficult to control. It is therefore most important to obtain reliable clean seed potatoes and to keep to a very strict rotation and not grow potatoes on the same piece of land for more than one year in three as a minimum rotation. If aphids are allowed to attack the crop, they can spread virus, and so should be controlled at first sight. Potato blight sprays based on copper need to be applied regularly in southern and western areas, which are the regions most affected. Crops in other areas should be sprayed after humid conditions have prevailed. Warnings of likely imminent potato blight infections are given out over the radio in farming broadcasts. This is the time to spray, so that the fungicide forms a protective film to prevent the disease entering the plant tissues.

 Irrigation is important once the tubers are beginning to swell and in dry years will increase yield considerably.

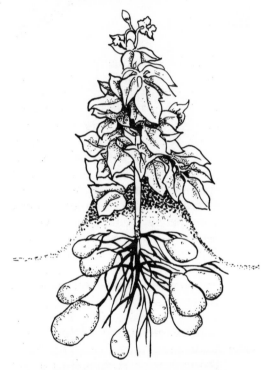

 Potatoes should be earthed up when the tops are 150 mm high or if there is a frost warning during May. Earthing up will help to stop the tubers pushing out of the ground and so turning green. It will also help to control germinating annual weed if the earthing-up is done three times at regular intervals until the foliage meets between the rows.

Root Group

Beetroot

One of the easiest of crops to grow, provided it is not sown too early.

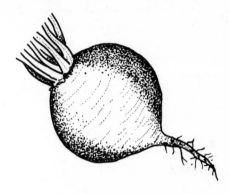

 The earliest crops of beetroot can usually be harvested at the beginning of July using early varieties, and a succession can continue with storage until the next March. Beetroot should not be left in the ground after December—severe frost can damage the roots.

 (a) No B.O.M. or compost is required.
(b) Apply 85 g per sq m of general compound fertiliser.
(c) No top dressing is necessary.

 The soil temperature at 100 mm should be 5°C (41°F) before sowing takes place or the crop is likely to run to seed. Sow 14 seeds per 300 mm, with 300 mm between rows. The beetroot seed is a multiple seed and so the crop always needs thinning; as soon as the seedlings can be handled, thin them to 50 mm apart in the rows. The best size roots for eating are 50–75 mm in diameter so main crops need not be sown until the end of May or even June in favoured areas.

 Yield is approximately 2.25 kg per m run of single row.

 No particular pests or diseases.

 There should be no need to irrigate but it will not harm the crop and will increase the yield.

Carrots

 A succession of fresh roots can be harvested from June until December (the late maincrop varieties may be left in the soil all winter but they are liable to attack from slugs in particular and if the weather is very severe they cannot be lifted). Almost all the rest of the year can be covered by storage.

 (a) No B.O.M. or compost is required.
(b) Apply 85 g per sq m of general compound fertiliser.
(c) No top dressing is required.

 Direct sowing is necessary as carrots cannot be transplanted. They are best grown in beds unless really large carrots are required. For the bed system sow six rows 100–150 mm apart and then leave 450–600 mm for access before starting the next

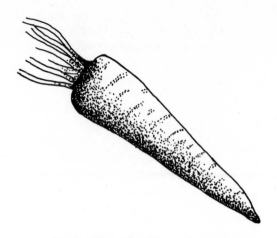

bed. The number of seeds per metre run of row should be approximately 80. This system works very well for finger-type carrots, but for larger carrots the rows should be 300 mm apart and the seed sown at 60 seeds per metre run, the plants being thinned as soon as they can be handled to 50 mm apart. Early varieties should be sown in March, maincrop varieties April–May and early varieties once again in June-early July to follow an earlier crop of some other vegetable.

 Early varieties will yield 2.5 kg per m run of single row, main-crop varieties 3.75–4.5 kg per m run of single row.

 Carrot fly is by far the worst problem. This can be controlled by Diazinon granules applied to the soil before or during sowing and is available in amateur packs. For sowings made between April and July it is almost essential to use the chemical to prevent attack, even then late attacks when the chemical has dispersed in October, November and December can severely damage the crop. To avoid this it is better to harvest the crop in late October-November and store it. Rotation will also help prevent a build-up of the pest.

 Irrigation will increase yield in periods of drought.

 This is a crop which will not stand any compaction. Only a light firming should be carried out when preparing the seedbed.

Parsnips

 Parsnips come from the same family as carrots but are a tougher longer-growing crop and are normally only used during the winter. The season is October-March.

 (a) No B.O.M. or compost should be dug in.
(b) Apply 85 g per sq m of general compound fertiliser.
(c) No top dressing is required.

 Like carrots, parsnips must be sown direct as they cannot be transplanted. Sow from March to early May in rows 400 mm apart, approximately 40 seeds per m run, and thin when the seedlings can be handled to 75 mm between plants.

 Yield is approximately 6.75 kg per m run.

 Sometimes carrot fly will attack this crop but the damage is not so great as on carrots. Any control is difficult because of the length of growing season the crop requires. If you know that carrot fly does attack in your area, sowing can be delayed until early May to avoid the first attack and Diazinon used as for carrots. This will produce slightly smaller roots.

 Irrigation is not necessary.

 Seed from this crop cannot be kept; fresh must be bought every year.

Salad Group

Lettuce

Lettuce is a relatively easy crop, and there are many different varieties to choose from. It is well worth growing even in the smallest vegetable plot.

 It is normally possible to provide a succession of lettuce from March/April in the south or April/May in the north until November or the first severe frosts. Moderate frost will not normally damage growing plants.

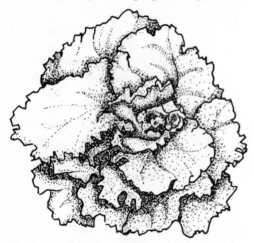

 (a) Dig in rotted B.O.M. or compost, up to 20 kg per sq m.
(b) Apply 85 g per sq m of basic compound fertiliser plus 35 g per sq m of the N-only fertiliser. If a second sowing on the same area of land is carried out the N fertiliser only should be applied again, in the same amount as before. The N fertiliser should not be applied for overwintering crops.
(c) No top dressing is required.

 There are many different varieties, taking varying lengths of time to maturity. A succession during the summer may be achieved in one of two ways: by choosing one or two varieties that take roughly the same time to mature and making sowings every 10 or 14 days, or by choosing two or three varieties that take different lengths of time to mature, and sowing them all on the same day. This can be repeated about three weeks later so that the quickest to mature of the second batch follows the slowest variety of the first batch, and so on.

Those maturing in autumn and spring are much more dependent on prevailing temperatures and succession is more difficult to achieve—nothing can be done about the tricks and abnormalities of the weather. A mature head of lettuce in spring or autumn, when the weather is cooler, will hold for considerably longer than in the warmer summer months so that fewer sowings are required for autumn and spring. Lettuce are very highly bred, different varieties being suited to different seasons, so when choosing a variety ensure it is right for the time of year.

Lettuce may be grown as follows:

(a) Sow in the autumn to overwinter and mature in spring.
(b) Sow in October—November in the cold frame, where the seedlings overwinter, and then plant outside.
(c) Sow in January—February in the cold frame to plant out in

the spring.

(d) Sow outside in March to mature in June.

(e) Sow from April until June in succession for summer crops.

(f) Sow in late June-July for autumn crops.

The spacing requirements vary from 175 mm each way for small varieties up to 300 mm each way for large varieties. Lettuce should always be planted firmly but with 6–12 mm of stem showing above the soil surface— never plant too deeply, it causes several problems.

Below is an example of how a succession of lettuce may be obtained, using butterhead-type varieties.

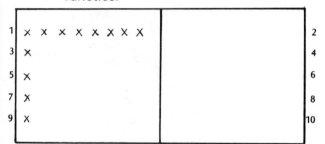

The plot is 1.25 m × 4 m, divided into 10 rows with eight plants per row, the planting distance being 250 mm each way, with half that distance at the edges of the plot. The sequence of cropping may be as follows, using the correct variety for the season:

Row (1) Sow in October in the frame; plant in March; harvest in May.

Row (2) Sow in the frame at the end of February; plant in March; harvest in late May.

Row (3) Sow in the open at the end of March (in the frame in the north), then plant out in April; harvest in June.

Row (4) Sow in the open in mid-April; harvest at the end of June.

Row (5) Sow in the open at the end of April; harvest at the beginning of July.

Row (6) Sow in the open in early May; harvest in mid-July.

Row (7) Sow in the open at the end of May; harvest at the end of July.

Row (8) Sow in the open in early June; harvest in early August.

Row (9) Sow in the open at the end of June; harvest at the end of August.

Row (10) Sow in the open in early July; harvest in early to mid-September.

Row (11) Sow in the open in mid-July; harvest in late September.

Row (12) Sow in the open at the end of July; harvest in mid-October.

 Taking 12 crops off the plot of land described above, and allowing two losses for each crop, 72 lettuces may be produced between May and October. This works out at approximately three lettuces per week. Because of the unpredictable weather the first three or four sowings may reach maturity very close together, and it may be that only every other one of these early sowings is required.

 In the late summer and autumn, lettuce suffer from **mildew**, so at that time of year it is best to use the varieties that are resistant to mildew. A spray containing Benumyl will also give some control.

Lettuce root aphid feeds on the roots; the plants look as if they need water even when the soil is moist, and the lower leaves turn yellow. When the roots are pulled up white cotton-wool-like patches can be seen to cover them. The aphids' other host is Lombardy Poplar. Prevention is by applying granules containing Diazinon to the soil before sowing.

 Irrigation is beneficial until the heart is forming, but in hot weather irrigation on the heart may make it rot.

 Spring and summer lettuce is a quick-growing crop, and rotation is not so very important, so the early or late sowings (particularly if the plants are raised in containers and then planted out) can often be grown before or after other crops.

Ridge Cucumbers

Despite their dependence on the weather, ridge cucumbers are generally an easy crop to grow, and the new hybrids are very sweet and pleasant to eat.

 Ridge cucumbers are susceptible to frost and are therefore grown between June and the autumn,

the cropping season being from July until the first frost. Two plants are usually required to give a satisfactory succession.

 (a) Dig in B.O.M. or compost up to 20 kg per sq m.
(b) Apply 85 g per sq m of basic compound fertiliser plus 70 g per sq m of the N-only fertiliser.
(c) Top dressing should not be necessary.

 To gain the maximum growing season, sow the seeds in the frame in mid-May, planting out after the chance of frost is passed. One plant requires at least 0.8 sq m.

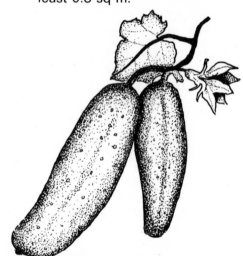

 Once cropping has commenced and if the cucumbers are cut regularly each plant should produce about one per week.

 There are no particular pests or diseases.

 Water as the young fruits begin to swell.

Ridge cucumbers do better in warm dry summers. Too much rain tends to cause the fruits to damp off.

Outdoor Tomatoes

Outdoor tomatoes are something of a gamble but in recent years several very good varieties have been bred, and they are always worth a try if space is available.

 The crop is susceptible to frost, so planting usually takes place in June and the fruits ripen from September onwards, each plant providing its own natural succession.

 (a) Dig in B.O.M. or compost up to 20 kg per sq m.
(b) Apply 85 g per sq m of basic compound fertiliser plus 35 g per sq m of N-only fertiliser.
(c) No top dressing is required.

 Sow in a pot in sterilised compost in the second week of April. Cover the pot with a sheet of glass inside the frame until the seedlings emerge and then remove the sheet of glass. Prick the seedlings off as soon as they can be handled into 90 mm pots, using sterilised compost, one per pot; keep the frame closed during this time, ventilating only on the warmest days. Grow on in the frame until the first flower opens into full bloom; then harden off. Plant out in about mid-June with a cane for support,

leaving 450 mm between the plants.

 Yield cannot be given accurately because it is so dependent on the weather. However, the fruits that do not ripen before the first frosts are due but are mature may be stored in a shed or kitchen to ripen, and the immature fruits can be used as chutney.

 There are no particular pests or diseases.

 Once the plants are established after planting out, irrigation should not be necessary.

 Many outdoor tomatoes are bush varieties and thus require no training, but the fruits drag on the floor. It is therefore wise to put straw under them for protection. If you are growing non-bush varieties, the side-shoots should be pinched off as shown.

Metrication

Note: the metric measurements given in the text have been rounded off to make application easier

LENGTH

mm	in
12	0.5
25	1.0
75	3.0
100	3.9
200	7.9
300	11.8
400	15.7
500	19.7
600	23.6
700	27.6
800	31.5
900	35.4
1000	39.4

1000 millimetres (mm) = 1 metre (m)

m	ft	in
1	3	3
2	6	7
3	9	11
4	13	1
5	16	5
6	19	8
7	22	11
8	26	3
9	29	6
10	32	8
15	49	3
20	65	7

WEIGHT

g	oz
25	0.9
50	1.8
75	2.6
100	3.5
200	7.1
300	10.6
400	14.1
500	17.6
1000	35.3

1000 grammes (g) = 1 kilogramme (kg)

kg	lb	oz
1	2	3
2	4	7
3	6	10
4	8	13
5	11	0
6	13	4
7	15	7
8	17	10
9	19	13
10	22	1
15	33	1
20	44	1

AREA

1000 sq cm = 155 sq in
1 sq m = 10.8 sq ft

Where amounts per square metre of compost or fertiliser are given for each vegetable, the equivalent rates per square yard are as follows:

35 g per sq m = 1 oz per sq yd
50 g per sq m = 1½ oz per sq yd
70 g per sq m = 2 oz per sq yd
85 g per sq m = 2½ oz per sq yd
20 kg per sq m = 1 cwt per sq yd